FACILITATING THE INTEGRATION OF LEARNING

FACILITATING THE INTEGRATION OF LEARNING

Five Research-Based Practices to Help College Students Connect Learning Across Disciplines and Lived Experience

James P. Barber

Foreword by Kate McConnell

First published 2020 by Stylus Publishing, LLC.

First Edition, 2020

Published 2023 by Routledge
605 Third Avenue, New York, NY 10017
4 Park Square, Milton Park, Abingdon, Oxon OX14 4RN

Routledge is an imprint of the Taylor & Francis Group, an informa business

Copyright © 2020 Taylor & Francis Group.

All rights reserved. No part of this book may be reprinted or reproduced or utilised in any form or by any electronic, mechanical, or other means, now known or hereafter invented, including photocopying and recording, or in any information storage or retrieval system, without permission in writing from the publishers.

Notice:
Product or corporate names may be trademarks or registered trademarks, and are used only for identification and explanation without intent to infringe.

Library of Congress Cataloging-in-Publication Data
Names: Barber, James P. (Senior associate dean for academic programs), author.
Title: Facilitating the integration of learning : five research-based practices to help college students connect learning across disciplines and lived experience / James P. Barber ; foreword by Kate McConnell.
Description: Sterling, Virginia : Stylus, [2020] | Includes bibliographical references and index.
Identifiers: LCCN 2020043433 | ISBN 9781620367483 (paperback) | ISBN 9781620367476 (hardcover)
Subjects: LCSH: College student development programs. | Interdisciplinary approach in education. | Experiential learning.
Classification: LCC LB2343.4 .B37 2020 | DDC 378.1/98--dc23
LC record available at https://lccn.loc.gov/2020043433

ISBN 13: 978-1-62036-747-6 (hbk)
ISBN 13: 978-1-62036-748-3 (pbk)
ISBN 13: 978-1-00-344477-0 (ebk)

DOI: 10.4324/9781003444770

*For Carin,
Lucy, and Charlie*

CONTENTS

FOREWORD ix
Kate McConnell

ACKNOWLEDGMENTS xiii

INTRODUCTION 1

PART ONE: HOW STUDENTS INTEGRATE LEARNING AND WHY THEY MUST

1 FALSE BORDERS
  The Case for Integrative Learning 9

2 INTEGRATION OF LEARNING MODEL 24

3 REFLECTION
  The Foundation of Integration 37

PART TWO: HOW YOU CAN HELP: CREATING EXPERIENCES TO FACILITATE INTEGRATION OF LEARNING

4 PRACTICE 1
  Mentoring Students 51

5 PRACTICE 2
  Writing as Praxis 65

6 PRACTICE 3
  Encourage Juxtaposition 79

7 PRACTICE 4
  Hands-On Experiences 92

8 PRACTICE 5
  Embrace Diversity and Identity 105

PART THREE: HOW TO MAKE IT STICK

9 CREATING AN INTEGRATIVE CURRICULUM 123

10 DOCUMENTING AND ASSESSING INTEGRATION OF LEARNING 137

APPENDIX A
Additional Details on Learning, Development, and Meaning for Those
Who Care to Read It 149

APPENDIX B
Student Examples 153

REFERENCES 155

INDEX 165

FOREWORD

With its 2018 report, *The Integration of the Humanities and Arts with Sciences, Engineering, and Medicine in Higher Education: Branches from the Same Tree*, the National Academies of Science, Engineering, and Medicine lamented that

> although integrative programs and initiatives have been studied for their relationship to learning outcomes . . . very few scholars have examined what students are integrating or how participation in these programs and initiatives helps students with the integrative process (i.e., how these students are bringing together information). Rather, scholars assume that integration is occurring as a result of students' participation in these programs and initiatives and suggest that associations between participation and learning outcomes are based on the assumed integration occurring. (p 82)

In other words, the predominant, *a priori* assumption is that if colleges and universities simply create curricular structures or thematically organize course content under the auspices of "integration," the desired learning occurs. With this book, James P. Barber challenges that assumption, leveraging empirical evidence from the Wabash National Study of Liberal Arts Education, one of the more robust longitudinal studies measuring the cognitive and developmental impact of what the Association of American Colleges & Universities (AAC&U) refers to as a *liberal education*. Coupled with a truly optimistic and growth-minded orientation, Barber asserts that from the beginning students are indeed practicing integration of learning; however, they are doing so without our help and acknowledgment, if not in spite of us.

This volume balances theory, data, and praxis to create a readily understandable model for the integration of learning that transcends the curricular and cocurricular divide. As an educational psychologist, I was particularly appreciative of his succinct and helpful interpretation of the commonalities and points of contrast between the learning sciences, with its focus on cognitive processing, and models of development from the worlds of student affairs and adult learning. He positions integration of learning as an outcome as worthy and complex as another "holy grail" of educational research—transfer—and builds on what we know of metacognition, motivation, and self-regulation to translate his empirical observations from the Wabash National Study into his three-pronged understanding of students' ability to integrate characterized by increasing complexity, from establishing connections, to application of knowledge, to the synthesis of a new whole.

It is one thing to posit a new framework or theory for college student learning and development, it is another to provide pragmatic, scalable strategies for promoting and assessing student learning. Integrative learning—connecting relevant experiences and academic knowledge; seeing and making connections across disciplines and perspectives; adapting and applying skills, abilities, theories, or methodologies gained in one situation to new situations; communicating in language that demonstrates cross-disciplinary fluency; and demonstrating a developing sense of self as a learner, building on prior experiences to respond to new and challenging contexts (AAC&U, 2010)—does not spontaneously occur in the classroom or cocurriculum. Indeed, it is likely the case that our default epistemological orientations and pedagogical approaches hinder students' ability to connect, apply, and synthesize across courses, disciplines, and experiences. It is in this space that this volume holds great promise for educators.

The five research-based practices delineated—mentoring, , the centrality of written reflection, encouraging the juxtaposition of ideas and arguments, providing relevant hands-on experiences, and embracing diversity and identity—transcend disciplinary differences and organizational silos. The practices are amenable to scaffolding and scaling and can be designed to provide students with learning opportunities ranging from introductory to the more complex. Ideally, all learners would have access to purposefully designed opportunities to integrate throughout their undergraduate career, flexing this cognitive muscle early, often, and with increased sophistication across classes and the cocurriculum, as well as within the unscripted spaces of their world of friends and family and as their future selves in community and work.

Importantly, Barber's positioning of integrative learning as a desirable, attainable, and assessable student learning outcome holds the promise of *making all of us who say we value it accountable for its delivery.* The question then becomes one effort and investment, of rethinking our past practices, of retooling our approaches. Because, as Mary Taylor Huber (2020) writes, "at stake, of course, is the willingness of colleges and universities to recognize and support teaching—and inquiry into teaching and learning—as essential to meeting their liberal education goals" (p. vii). With resources like this, I remain decidedly optimistic about the academy's ability to do just that—recognize and support the very teaching that inculcates the habits of mind necessary for our students and our graduates to connect, apply, and synthesize in our ever-increasingly complex world.

Kate McConnell
Assistant Vice President for Research and Assessment
Director of VALUE Institute
Office of Quality, Curriculum, and Assessment
Association of American Colleges & Universities

ACKNOWLEDGMENTS

My greatest acknowledgment is for my wife, Carin, who has been a constant source of support and inspiration through my research and writing this book.

Our children, Lucy and Charlie, have given me motivation to write this book in hopes that the colleges and universities they attend someday may promote integration of learning intentionally and enthusiastically.

I thank my parents, John and Julia Barber, for the value that they placed on education throughout my life. I am grateful for my sister, Jessica Rice, who endured many hours of playing school when we were growing up and was my very first student.

My mentors in this research, Patricia M. King and Marcia B. Baxter Magolda, served as the principal investigators for the qualitative portion of the Wabash National Study of Liberal Arts Education. I appreciate the original offer to join the research team as a first-year PhD student as well as their continued invitation to remain involved with the project.

The ideas in this book began with my doctoral dissertation at the University of Michigan. I am grateful to my dissertation committee members, Patricia King (chair), Marcia B. Baxter Magolda, Janet Lawrence, and the late Wilbert "Bill" McKeachie, for guiding my initial thinking about integration of learning.

I owe a debt to all of members of the Wabash National Study research team. Well over 50 interviewers, transcribers, and summarizers have contributed to the project since 2004. In particular, I am thankful to Carin Barber, Cassie Barnhardt, Marie Kendall Brown, Julie DeGraw, Lisa Landreman, Anat Levtov, Ramona Meraz Lewis, Nathan Lindsay, Rosie Perez, Ethan Stephenson, Woo-jeong Shim, Kari Taylor, JoNes VanHecke, Kerri Wakefield, and Kelley Walczak for their teamwork and support over the years. This project was originally funded by the Center of Inquiry in the Liberal Arts at Wabash College. I gratefully acknowledge the sponsorship of the Wabash National Study in support of this project.

I am thankful for the expertise of John von Knorring, president and publisher at Stylus Publishing, for believing in this book project and offering invaluable advice on how to best organize my ideas in this manuscript.

I appreciate the time and energy of those who offered advice on this book as it was in development. Daniel Bureau, Amber Garrison Duncan, Michelle Espino, Rosie Perez, Julie Posselt, and JoNes VanHecke each offered their insight and expertise as I wrote the initial book proposal and subsequent chapters. Special thanks to Paul Hanstedt for his thoughtful critique of the first full draft of the manuscript.

My colleagues at William & Mary in particular have offered a great deal of support for my work. I benefited from a research leave that allowed me to focus on writing the initial manuscript. My faculty colleagues Pamela Eddy and Gene Roche read early drafts of my work and offered insights and critique. I spent many hours in Swem Library working on drafts of the manuscript, and I want to acknowledge that this book benefited from several William & Mary faculty writers' retreats, cosponsored by William & Mary Libraries and the Office of the Provost.

I am fortunate to work with stellar graduate students at William & Mary who have helped move my thinking forward. I especially want to thank Amanda Armstrong and Johann Ducharme for their editorial and research support for this book. I also want to thank the members of the Integration of Learning Research Team who worked with me on several studies that contributed to the ideas in this book: Leslie Bohon, Justin Bruce, Billy Bush, Nancy Everson, Laura Feltman, Diana Hernández, Neal Holly, Sharon Stone, and Kristen Tarantino.

I benefited greatly from working with Katie Linder of Katie Linder Coaching. I participated in one of Katie's Virtual Writing Groups at a critical point when writing this manuscript. The accountability of the writing group and the follow-up coaching from Katie pushed me forward when I needed it.

Finally, I am grateful to the student participants of the Wabash National Study who shared their college experiences with us over 4 years. Without their generosity, this book would not be possible.

INTRODUCTION

What is the most powerful learning experience you had as a college student? I often start talks about integrative learning with this simple question, and the responses I get are remarkably similar. Very few people mention an academic course or an organization meeting. Even fewer describe a specific lecture or reading. Most often, people describe the types of integrative learning described in this book: educational experiences that cross boundaries and contexts and remain relevant years later. These learning experiences are visceral; people can often recall very specific details about whom they were with, what they were wearing, or how they felt in that moment. To integrate learning is to connect, apply, and synthesize knowledge and skills across contexts. The most powerful learning experiences we can provide in universities are those that prompt integration of learning.

In an analysis of nearly 200 interviews with student participants in the Wabash National Study of Liberal Arts Education (Barber, 2009, 2012), I found that students integrated learning often in concrete and abstract ways. However, in the vast majority of cases, students were integrating on their own or with their peers; a faculty member, student affairs professional, or other adult mentor was rarely mentioned. This book is designed to introduce college educators to the idea of integration of learning and provide guidance on how to promote and assess integration of learning.

The ability to integrate learning across contexts is a crucial outcome of higher education. In this book, I argue that as college educators we can help our students integrate learning better by explicitly and intentionally teaching them how to do so. It is necessary to be transparent about teaching integration of learning to your students. It's important to be up front in your work with students and tell them that integration of learning is an expectation of their participation in your course, program, or event. No matter the topic or semester, I include the following as a learning outcome in my syllabi: "Students will integrate their learning in this course with prior knowledge, experience, and skills." This is the central outcome of my work as an educator regardless of the context, which I unabashedly tell my students and colleagues.

My purpose for writing this book is to provide a guide for other college educators to help students integrate learning. I use the term *college educators* broadly to include those in teaching positions, student affairs administrators, athletic coaches, internship supervisors, and so on. I see an audience for this book in academic and student affairs work. The goal of integrating learning is to eliminate the false boundaries among contexts—in class and out of class, academic affairs and student affairs, disciplinary boundaries—so we must all be on the same page as college educators about what integration of learning is and how we can help students integrate learning better.

When I meet with groups of undergraduate students, I often start by telling them three things I want them to know about their own learning:

1. You are learning all the time, everywhere.
2. You already come to college with valuable knowledge.
3. You will be more successful in college (and in life) if you can integrate your learning.

These three items are important for college educators to consider as well.

Students are learning all the time, everywhere. We can't be limited in how we see learning as educators. Even though my main role as a faculty member is teaching students in my classroom, I need to be attuned to what they are learning outside my classroom because their experiences made a difference in how they learn in my class and vice versa; that is, what students are learning in my class has an impact on what they do and how they see things in other parts of their lives.

Students come to college with valuable knowledge. They usually have at least 17 years of life experience and 13-plus years of formal education. Students' prior knowledge is a valuable foundation, and college educators can leverage this prior knowledge to help students learn effectively in the university setting.

Students will be more successful in college and in life if they can integrate their learning. The ability to connect knowledge and skills from disparate contexts quickly and effectively allows students to make meaning of their curriculum as a whole rather than viewing coursework as a series of requirements and checkboxes. In addition, integration is an ability that is applicable and prized in virtually every career path a student may take after graduation.

To help college educators think about integration of learning, this book is organized in three main parts.

Part One: How Students Integrate Learning and Why They Must

The first part of this book introduces the idea of integration of learning and describes the integration of learning model that emerged from my research in the Wabash National Study (Barber 2009, 2012, 2014). These three chapters lay the foundation for the book and provide readers with the necessary information to help students integrate learning, what integration of learning is, how to promote it, and how to assess integrative learning.

In chapter 1, "False Borders: The Case for Integrative Learning," I argue why integration of learning is an essential outcome of higher education in the twenty-first century and describe the structural barriers in higher education to the very kind of learning we espouse to promote.

Chapter 2, "Integration of Learning Model," describes my theory of integration of learning. I use a grounded theory approach to analyze in-depth interviews with college students and discuss three approaches that students use to integrate learning. I detail the integration of learning model and the data from the Wabash National Study (King, Kendall Brown, Lindsay, & VanHecke, 2007; Pascarella & Blaich, 2013; Seifert, Goodman, King, & Baxter Magolda, 2010) the model is based on.

In chapter 3, "Reflection: The Foundation of Integration," I explore multiple forms of reflection and how the act of reflection provides the time and space to process one's experiences, allows one to consider the ways new information fits (or conflicts) with prior knowledge, and undergirds the meaning-making process.

Part Two: How You Can Help: Creating Experiences to Facilitate Integration of Learning

The second part of the book provides practical, real-world strategies for facilitating integration of learning that college educators can use right away. However, this section is not about specific contexts and environments. Particular contexts are used in examples, but the book is intentionally not organized to be context specific (e.g., classroom, residence hall, student organizations, etc.), which would be counter to the purpose of the book. I aim to help college educators facilitate student learning across contexts; therefore, I have not organized the book by contexts but rather by the key characteristics of five practices discussed in the next chapters.

In chapter 4, "Practice 1: Mentoring Students," I examine the importance of mentoring for integration of learning. Throughout the Wabash

National Study, we realized the impact of the interview as an intervention and the importance of the interaction of individuals.

Writing as a practice to promote integration of learning is pervasive in higher education. In chapter 5, "Practice 2: Writing as Praxis," I provide examples of formal writing assignments that call on students to integrate learning and examples of informal and personal writing to dispel the notion that formal academic writing is the only (or the best) route.

In chapter 6, "Practice 3: Encourage Juxtaposition," I examine experiences that deliberately encourage the juxtaposition of different perspectives and how those experiences promote integration of learning for students. Intentionally including diverse perspectives (texts, films, panelists, etc.) in an educational experience provides an opportunity for students to wrestle with dissonance and decide how conflicts might be reconciled.

In chapter 7, "Practice 4: Hands-On Experiences," I discuss experiences that promote integration of learning for college students that are often hands-on or immersive in nature, such as living-learning communities, study abroad, and maker spaces. By taking students out of their familiar surroundings and comfort zones and immersing them in a new and different context, students are challenged to reconcile new observations and ways of seeing the world with what's preciously known.

Simply stated, we learn better in diverse groups. In chapter 8, "Practice 5: Embrace Diversity and Identity," I provide strategies for college educators to embrace the diversity among their students and encourage students to bring their full identities into their education. Undergraduate students come to college with rich histories and complex identities, including prior knowledge that may be quite relevant to the learning at hand.

Part Three: How to Make It Stick

Over the course of chapters 4 through 8, I discuss five strategies to promote integration of learning for college students. Part Three focuses on weaving those strategies into educators' practices.

I use the word *curriculum* broadly; it might apply to a major, a single course, programming for a student organization, or an athletic team. Chapter 9, "Creating an Integrative Curriculum," brings together the practices from the preceding five chapters in a holistic matrix (Table 9.1) that educators can use in their own planning.

How do you know your students can integrate learning? Chapter 10, "Documenting and Assessing Integration of Learning," summarizes the main points of this book and emphasizes that the ultimate goal is not to create these integrative activities as one-off experiences but rather to teach students how to integrate learning so they can do it throughout their lives. In this chapter, I explain how to assess and document students' learning to provide them with feedback, demonstrate student mastery of the outcomes, maintain accreditation, and secure funding and human resources.

Appendix A, "Additional Details on Learning, Development, and Meaning for Those Who Care to Read It" is exactly what the title suggests. In this appendix, I go deeper into the background of integrative learning and how the research on this topic has evolved over the past century. I also detail aspects of the developmental model of self-authorship and how it related to integration of learning. This appendix is supplementary material for those who which to learn more about the underlying theories I reference in the book.

Appendix B, "Student Examples," is a listing of the student participants who are quoted throughout this book. One of the strengths of the Wabash National Study interview data is the diversity of the student sample, representing a variety of institutions, years in school, races, genders, and experiences. These students' voices are the heart of my research. This appendix provides readers with a compilation of students highlighted in this book.

This book captures the core tenets of my approach to higher education. I hope readers will find it insightful, relevant, and, most of all, practical in their work with students.

PART ONE

HOW STUDENTS INTEGRATE LEARNING AND WHY THEY MUST

I

FALSE BORDERS

The Case for Integrative Learning

College students spend up to 90% of their time outside the classroom in residence halls, at internship sites, on athletic fields, and in part-time or full-time employment. When they are not in the classroom, students lead busy lives, learning from student organizations, paid work, volunteer service, sports, and spending time with family and friends. For part-time or nontraditional students, this percentage may be even greater. So how does the learning that happens outside the classroom connect with what's going on inside the classroom? Too often, it doesn't, and college educators aren't skilled in helping students make these connections across contexts.

The borders in higher education are well established and heavily guarded. What happens inside a classroom is considered distinct from what occurs outside a classroom, and often learning is synonymous with the classroom experience. The borders continue in the campus community: academic affairs is a separate world from student affairs, and in academic affairs, an assortment of programs, departments, schools, and colleges further divide up the educational landscape and grant jurisdiction over specific content and credit. The content knowledge gained in the formal curriculum is compartmentalized, and typical classroom experiences fail to draw on students' experiences outside class nor their personal background characteristics. Likewise, cocurricular activities are often centered on events and outcomes in the real world apart from students' majors or courses. These are self-imposed, false borders.

Such structural barriers in academe stand as obstacles to the very kind of learning we espouse to promote as college educators. To be explicit, this book has a dual audience: those who work in academic affairs and those who work in student affairs. To diminish these boundaries and highlight our common purpose in serving students, I use the term *college educators* broadly to include faculty, student affairs professionals, coaches, and other administrators who work with students. Throughout this book, I provide examples from multiple contexts to speak to this bifurcated audience and to pull the curtain back a bit and show those in academic affairs the kind of work student affairs administrators do and vice versa. The way higher education institutions are organized promotes isolation, and as a result we don't often know how colleagues across campus (or across the hall) work with students on a day-to-day basis. We're all in this together, and in this book, I speak to educators in academic affairs, student affairs, and everywhere in between.

Students come to college with (at least) 17 years of life experience but are often treated as blank slates when they arrive on campus. They are left to make connections across contexts on their own, if at all. This presents a challenge and an opportunity for college educators because the ability to integrate learning quickly, efficiently, and across divergent contexts is highly valued by employers. In fact, I believe that integration of learning is an essential outcome of higher education in the twenty-first century. In an era when the relevance of a college degree is debated in U.S. society, and the cost of financing higher education is increasingly shifting to individual students and families, integration of learning is a coveted skill that enables students to put the knowledge and skills gained in the college experience to immediate use in other contexts.

The knowledge economy and rapidly changing nature of work in today's world require individuals to be adept at making learning connections across contexts. Many of the leading higher education and professional associations cite integration of learning as an essential learning outcome (e.g., Association of American Colleges & Universities, 2005, 2008, 2017; National Academies of Sciences, Engineering, and Medicine, 2018). Employer surveys also demonstrate the desire for college graduates to enter the workforce with the ability to apply what they learned in the college setting in the real world after graduation.

Without the ability to integrate learning, graduates are at a severe disadvantage in the knowledge economy of the twenty-first century. However, most college educators have not been trained to promote integration of learning, leaving students to make connections on their own, if at all.

My Own Connection

I became interested in integration of learning when I was a university administrator, working in areas such as student organization advising and residence life. In student affairs, I met regularly with undergraduates to discuss their leadership roles, upcoming events, and (too often) the crises of the day. In these meetings with students, I witnessed them connect learning all the time, for example, using what they learned in their finance major to inform their role as treasurer of an organization or relating a lesson learned from family to addressing a relationship on campus. This kind of integration was common. I enjoyed seeing students make these links, and although I didn't have a name for it or a systematic approach to developing it, I encouraged this type of learning.

As a doctoral student and aspiring faculty member, I was fortunate to work as a graduate researcher with the Wabash National Study of Liberal Arts Education (King et al., 2007; Pascarella & Blaich, 2013; Seifert et al., 2010) and could finally could put a name to this idea: integration of learning. Integration of learning was one of seven educational outcomes in the study, along with leadership, well-being, inclination to inquire and lifelong learning, effective reasoning and problem-solving, moral character, and intercultural effectiveness. Integration of learning was the only outcome that was measured exclusively using qualitative methods.

The Wabash National Study is one of the largest qualitative studies of student learning and development undertaken. The research team collected 924 interviews from 315 students over the course of 4 years (Baxter Magolda & King, 2012). More than 50 researchers have been involved in data collection and analysis over 15 years (2004–2019) and counting. Although data collection ended in 2008–2009, analysis continues as of 2020. The data collected are invaluable in the study of college student learning writ large (including integration of learning). I am grateful to have worked with the Wabash National Study team from the beginning.

Through an analysis of nearly 200 in-depth interviews with undergraduates (Barber, 2012), I developed the following definition for *integration of learning*:

> Integration of learning is the demonstrated ability to connect, apply, and/or synthesize information coherently from disparate contexts and perspectives, and make use of these new insights in multiple contexts. This includes the ability to connect the domain of ideas and philosophies to the everyday experience, from one field of study or discipline to another, from the past to the present, between campus and community life, from one part to the whole, from the abstract to the concrete, among multiple identity roles—and vice versa. (p. 593)

Three approaches to integrating learning—connection, application, and synthesis—form the heart of the integration of learning model that I introduce in the next chapter. This model serves as a framework to think about how students make meaning and how educators can help them to do so better.

The world is changing around us at an unprecedented pace. The amount of information available to the average college student is far greater than it was a generation ago. We are constantly connected to this information and each other through the Internet and the ubiquitous smart devices we carry everywhere we go. It has become an expectation that we can quickly access information, interpret it, and integrate it with what we already know.

How to Use This Book

I intend this book to be a guide for college educators to help students integrate learning. I'm a boundary crosser in higher education. I have worked professionally in academic affairs as a faculty member and earlier in student affairs as an administrator. As a student affairs professional, I spent a great deal of time advising undergraduate students in one-on-one meetings and in larger organizations. In those meetings with student leaders, I often witnessed students connecting what they learned in different contexts. When I left my full-time position to pursue a PhD in education, I was drawn to study this integration of learning. I saw how students linked formal and informal experiences in multiple areas during college and was eager to learn more about this type of learning. I was disappointed to find there was little literature about this process of learning. Plenty was written about the virtues of interdisciplinary work, liberal learning, and high-impact practices for higher education, but research on the process of integrating learning was scarce. I wanted to know more about how students integrated learning, and I set out to do so in my own research.

What I found in my analysis of interviews with students from the Wabash National Study was that students were integrating learning often in concrete and abstract ways. This was somewhat surprising, despite my personal experiences witnessing these moments of connection, because so much of the educational literature stressed the lack of integrated learning in college. However, in the vast majority of cases, students were integrating on their own or with their peers; students rarely mentioned a faculty member, student affairs professional, or other adult mentor. I designed this book to introduce the idea of integration of learning and provide a framework for how to promote and assess integration of learning.

Comments from the Wabash National Study participants illustrate concepts throughout the book to keep student voices centered. (Because of the longitudinal nature of the Wabash National Study, some of the quotes from student interviews have appeared in prior publications.) A full list of examples is included in Appendix B. Integration can be an abstract idea, and the examples from undergraduates' experiences help make it tangible. For example, Fran, a first-year student at pseudonymous Hudson College, described connections that spanned long periods of time and bridged in-class and out-of-class experiences. In this excerpt, Fran talked about integrating learning by making connections among her courses as well as with her experience living abroad in Brazil as an exchange student in high school:

> Just connecting two things in my classes that supposedly would have nothing to do with each other. Like my literature class, that freshman year symposium, what this essay's for, and we're reading Plato right now, and I'm taking another class called Race and Ethnicity in Brazil, and . . . we're talking about Plato and . . . it just so happens that we just finished a book that had a section on that and now I'm able to connect that . . . "Oh, I can see how we got the idea from this and now I can write about them both in my paper." It's just like I never thought about that. Who would've thought Plato and I could connect those—I don't know. That's what I'm saying . . . the classes can go together. . . . I thought they were so unrelated, but they're not. (Fran, Hudson College, Year 1)

In this example, Fran connected several experiences, studying Plato in two different classes in two semesters as well as connecting her class on Brazil to her experience living there as an exchange student later in the conversation. The Wabash National Study interviews are replete with examples of integration of learning, and we meet several students and learn about their college experiences throughout this book.

Despite growing enthusiasm for integration of learning, college educators are not especially skilled at helping students integrate their learning. Most university faculty and student affairs administrators are trained to be experts in their specific areas and do not know how to help students integrate learning, leaving students to make those connections independently. Even so, it's happening: Students are integrating learning all the time. However, college educators are missing a prime opportunity to help our students integrate sooner and gain lifelong habits of mind that enable them to intentionally integrate learning during college and beyond.

Integrating Definitions

Part of the problem is that educators do not have a shared language about this kind of learning. Several terms commonly used to discuss the general concept—*integrative, interdisciplinary, connected, experiential*—are related to one another, and I next explain their subtleties and illustrate how they are positioned with respect to each other.

Since the 1990s, the term *integration* has gained popularity in U.S. higher education to describe the idea of making connections and applying learning in multiple contexts (Association of American Colleges & Universities, 2002; Brown Leonard, 2007; Huber & Hutchings, 2004; Joint Task Force on Student Learning, 1998). However, the concept of making connections in learning is not new. Newman (1852) wrote, "I have said that all branches of knowledge are connected together, because the subject-matter of knowledge is intimately united in itself, as being the acts and the work of the Creator" (p. 99). More than 150 years later, the term *integration* was used increasingly to describe this idea of connected learning and has gained attention as an important outcome of a college education in the United States (Huber & Hutchings, 2004; Leskes, 2004).

The Association of American Colleges & Universities (AAC&U, 2002) called for higher education institutions to develop students as "integrative thinkers who can see connections in seemingly disparate information and draw on a wide range of knowledge to make decisions" (p. 21). Other educators suggested that integrative learning should one day "take its rightful place alongside breadth and depth as a hallmark of a quality undergraduate education" (Leskes, 2004, p. iv). Before we dive deeper into what integration of learning is and how we can help students do it better, we must first look at how it's defined and discussed.

Institutions, faculty, and students employ the language of integration inconsistently, which further complicates matters (DeZure, Babb, & Waldmann, 2005). This is not a new problem; Hopkins (1937) expressed much the same frustration with the lack of common terminology in education:

> With increasing frequency and with expanding meaning, the noun integration, or one of its grammatical associates, has been used during the past ten years [1927–1937] to designate educational goals, processes, and outcomes. . . . The result has led to confusion rather than to clarity of thinking on educational problems. That the word has met a need for which educators have been groping seems generally agreed. The problem now is to examine these divergent meanings and uses in light of accumulating

experiences so as to refine thinking in these areas, in order to better direct projected changes in present curriculum practices. (p. 1)

Integrative Practices

Despite the confusion created by a lack of common terminology of integration, convergence occurred in the late 1990s and 2000s on the word *integrative*. The term *connected learning* was widely used in the early 1990s by the Association of American Colleges (AAC; 1991), now the AAC&U, to describe this same or a very similar concept:

> There are two ways, by no means unrelated, in which the term "connected learning" may be employed. The first refers to the capacity for constructing relationships among various modes of knowledge and curricular experiences, the capacity for relating academic learning from one context to another. The second refers to the capacity for relating academic learning to the wider world, to public issues and personal experience. In either case, connected learning means generalizing learning: learning that extends beyond the necessary boundaries of any major and takes seriously its potential translation beyond the limits of a course or program. (p. 14)

One sign of the flux in use of this term is the variability of terms used, even within organizations. Specifically, the AAC&U has moved from *connected learning* (AAC, 1991) to *intentional learning* (AAC&U, 2002), and then to *integrative learning* (AAC&U & Carnegie Foundation, 2004), which is defined as follows:

> Integrative learning comes in many varieties: connecting skills and knowledge from multiple sources and experiences; applying theory to practice in various settings; utilizing diverse and even contradictory points of view; and, understanding issues and positions contextually. Significant knowledge within individual disciplines serves as the foundation, but integrative learning goes beyond academic boundaries. Indeed, integrative experiences often occur as learners address real-world problems, unscripted and sufficiently broad to require multiple areas of knowledge and multiple modes of inquiry, offering multiple solutions and benefiting from multiple perspectives. (para. 2)

Brown Leonard (2007) supported this positioning of *integrative practices* as an overarching term inclusive of many types of activities capturing "a variety of integrative forms such as interdisciplinary study, service-learning, experiential learning, cooperative learning, and the blending of in class and out of class learning that could occur in almost any context (e.g., classrooms, student organizations, residence halls, work)" (p. 13). Thus, *integrative practice* is the broadest of these related terms (Klein, 2005) and serves as an umbrella term for structures, strategies, and activities that bridge various divides, such as high school and college, general education and the major, introductory and advanced levels, experiences inside and outside the classroom, theory and practice, and disciplines and fields.

Interdisciplinarity is a subset of integrative practices (see Figure 1.1) that fosters connections among disciplines and interdisciplinary fields (Klein, 2005; Newell, 2007). Berger (1972) defined *interdisciplinary* as

> an adjective describing the interaction among two or more different disciplines. This interaction may range from simple communication of ideas to the mutual integration of organizing concepts, methodology, procedures, epistemology, terminology, data, and organization of research and education in a fairly large field. (pp. 25–26)

Therefore, an interdisciplinary group consists of people trained in different fields of knowledge (disciplines) with different concepts, methods, and

Figure 1.1. Positioning of definitions related to *integration of learning* as a collegiate educational outcome.

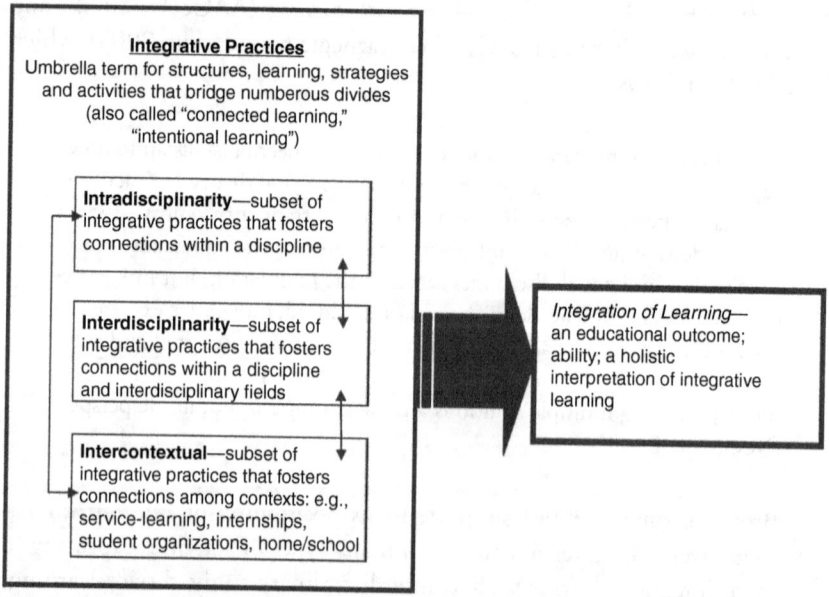

Note. From Barber (2009, p. 5).

data and terms organized to address a common problem with continuous intercommunication among the participants from the various disciplines. Interdisciplinarity is just one type of many possible subsets of integrative practices, each with differing levels of interaction between disciplines and actors (Haynes, 2005; Klein, 2005; Lattuca, 2001).

Another common variation is intradisciplinarity, which is contained within one discipline. Other variations include *adisciplinarity*, which describes a theme (e.g., thirst or time) that does not refer to disciplines in a traditional sense; *multidisciplinarity*, which describes the juxtaposition of various disciplines, sometimes without a connection between them; *pluridisciplinarity*, which includes the juxtaposition of disciplines assumed to be more or less related; and *transdisciplinarity*, which involves establishing a common system of axioms for a set of disciplines (Berger, 1972).

Like Berger (1972), Lattuca (2001) eliminated integration from her definition of *interdisciplinarity* altogether, opting to define this term instead as "the interaction of different disciplines" (p. 78). She reasoned that although integration is a goal of interdisciplinarity, measuring the level of integration in a course or project is difficult if not impossible to accomplish, so it's a challenging construct to use. She pointed out that some forms of integrative practice, such as transdisciplinarity, are more concerned with transcending disciplines than integrating them, and thus integration should not be a defining characteristic of interdisciplinarity. Based on her national study of interdisciplinary curricula, Lattuca focused on the types of questions asked, rather than the level of integration, to define *interdisciplinarity*. It is clear in this conceptualization that integration and interaction are not equivalent. In this light, interdisciplinary work is an interaction, whereas integration of learning suggests something more intimate, where individuals or ideas come together (integrate) rather than simply interact.

Fischer's (1980) skill theory presented a framework for understanding the increasing cognitive complexity indicative of integration of learning. This theory suggested that as people develop into adulthood, they have an escalating number of ways to make connections among the discrete facts that make up their knowledge base and lived experience. The increasing complexity of Fischer's skill theory has been illustrated by Kitchener and Fischer (1990) in a series of drawings progressing from a single dot, representing concrete concepts, to a line drawn between two dots to a square formed with four lines to a cube connecting six squares, and so on as the level of abstraction among the connections increases.

Just as there are many routes for connecting the dots in Fischer's (1980) theory as the level of abstraction increases, there are multiple potential pathways to integration of learning. Interdisciplinarity suggests one mechanism, employing two distinct disciplines to solve a problem rather than a synthesis of two or more areas or fields (e.g., biology and chemistry, as opposed to biochemistry), for achieving integration of learning. King and VanHecke (2006) applied Fischer's skill theory to student development and clarified that "cocurricular as well as curricular learning contexts offer many rich opportunities for students to learn and practice skills associated with making connections. . . . Developing these skills improves students' capacity to function in a complex world" (p. 16). This statement emphasized the point that the study of integration of learning as a collegiate outcome should take into consideration student experiences broadly, investigating learning in the disciplines (Schwartz & Fischer, 2006) and among disciplines (interdisciplinary), with a keen interest in the cocurriculum (intercontextual).

Transfer

Transfer of learning as a body of knowledge is concerned with how individuals think about ideas, beliefs, and information; it is centered on how people know and apply knowledge. Many refer to it simply as *transfer*. This term is more prevalent in research involving K–12 education and learning than it is in the higher education literature.

I argue that the language and theoretical concepts that constitute the transfer literature can be applied to a holistic study of integration of learning. As King and Baxter Magolda (1996) noted, "How individuals construct knowledge and use their knowledge is closely tied to their sense of self" (p. 166). That is, meaning-making (or how we see and make sense of the world) and identity (or how we see and present ourselves) are linked. For example, a person could apply what they have learned in one identity or role and apply it to another role, such as applying what a man has learned about being a supportive husband to being a supportive colleague. Conversely, an individual may find it difficult to progress to more complex ways of thinking about knowledge if their main priority is pleasing others or is fearful of others' judgment.

Despite the similar terminology, there is an important distinction between transfer and integration of learning: Transfer is applying the skills and knowledge from one context to another, whereas integration of learning involves connecting ideas and concepts and applying knowledge across contexts as well as synthesizing knowledge, making decisions about its relevance, and incorporating the selected skills and knowledge into one's established belief system or perspective. As such, integration of learning is a more complex, iterative version of transfer.

Integrative Processes

The practices described here facilitate the process of integration of learning. I see integration of learning as a process and educational outcome, as opposed to a practice for achieving said outcome, based on the premise that intellectual study should connect in meaningful ways to everyday life (AAC&U, 2002; King et al., 2007). My interpretation is that this involves the ability to successfully connect, apply, and synthesize information gathered from multiple sources and contexts over time for negotiating the everyday complexities of modern life. This construct includes the ability to integrate one's learning into a larger framework and a frame of reference for making meaning from the information and knowledge one possesses. Douglas (1992) described this integrative framework as

> the mucilage to hold together the information they [students] do possess. The framework is at one and the same time something that the student has created for himself or herself and a set of shared values, a disposition to understand, evaluate, and stand open to the ideas of others. (p. 197)

This ability, or outcome, has received much attention as of late and is also identified as a primary aim of a college education by the AAC&U and Carnegie Foundation (2004): "Fostering students' abilities to integrate learning—over time, across courses, and between academic, personal, and community life—is one of the most important goals and challenges of higher education" (p. 1).

Historical Development of Integrative Practice in Education

The history of integrative practice in U.S. higher education is in fact a tale of gradual *dis*integration. Until the late 1800s, curricula in U.S. colleges and universities were more cohesive than today, with most institutions favoring a common curriculum for students (AAC, 1991). The Yale Report of 1828 defended the common curriculum of the time, stating,

> But why, it is asked, should all the students in a college be required to tread in the same steps? Why should not each one be allowed to select those branches of study which are most to his taste, which are best adapted to his peculiar talents, and which are most nearly connected with his intended profession? To this we answer, that our prescribed course contains those subjects only which ought to be understood, as we think, by every one who aims at a thorough education. (Collegiate Way, 2016, p. 18)

However, U.S. higher education largely went in a different direction, focusing on disciplines, majors, and credit hours. The major was first introduced in U.S. institutions of higher education 50 years after the Yale Report (Collegiate Way, 2016), when Johns Hopkins University adopted majors as a means of allowing specialization in undergraduate studies in 1878 (AAC, 1991). Just four years later, the University of Michigan was the first institution to end the use of common examinations for each class of students. In 1882 the university discontinued its comprehensive exams in favor of testing in each discipline under the jurisdiction of faculty members and departments. This was the beginning of an increasing trend toward specialization that characterizes most higher educational institutions in the United States today (Levine, 1998). Historian John Higham argued that the contemporary academy is like "a house in which the inhabitants are leaning out of the many open windows gaily chatting with the neighbors, while the doors between the rooms stay closed" (AAC, 1991, p. 15). Ever since this trend toward specialization began, educators have been trying to reverse it in favor of a more holistic experience. Educational theorist Alfred Whitehead (1929) wrote extensively about the lack of integration in American education resulting from disciplinary divides. He suggested a unified curriculum, which he called simply "Life":

> The solution which I am urging, is to eradicate the fatal disconnection of subjects which kills the vitality of our modern curriculum. There is only one subject-matter for education, and that is Life in all its manifestations. Instead of this single unity, we offer children—Algebra, from which nothing follows; Geometry, from which nothing follows; Science, from which nothing follows; a Couple of Languages, never mastered; and lastly, most dreary of all, Literature, represented by the plays of Shakespeare, with philological notes and short analyses of plot and character to be in substance committed to memory. (pp. 10–11)

Other likeminded educators and researchers over the years have supported this idea, including some of the most influential educational scholars and researchers of the past century. Famed educational reformer John Dewey (1938) was an advocate for experiential education:

> A primary responsibility of educators is that they not only be aware of the general principle of the shaping of actual experience by environing conditions, but that they also recognize in the concrete what surroundings are conducive to having experiences that lead to growth. Above all, they should know how to utilize the surroundings, physical and social, that exist so as

to extract from them all that they have to contribute to building up experiences that are worthwhile. (p. 35)

The American Council on Education (1937) represented an early attempt by student affairs administrators to define their profession and role in student learning and positioned student affairs professionals as information curators, assembling and distributing information to students, but stopping short of including them as educators in their own right (Barber & Bureau, 2012).

Freire (1970) shared Dewey's progressive view of education and pursued experiential learning in his own work as an educator and activist. Freire advanced the notion of education as a community activity, in which essential knowledge is transmitted through daily experience. He disavowed traditional education, which he called the "banking concept of education" (p. 61) and regarded students as empty vessels into which knowledge should be deposited by the authority. Instead, he pressed for the student to be included as a cocreator of knowledge along with the teacher, acknowledging the prior learning and experience of each student as valuable and worthy to be shared.

A half century later, Boyer (1987) called for an "integrated core" for undergraduate general education:

> We conclude that general education urgently needs a new breath of life. More coherence is required to relate the core program to the lives of students and to the world they are inheriting. There is a need for students to go beyond their separate interests and gain a more integrated view of knowledge and a more authentic view of life. (p. 90)

Boyer (1990) also called for the recognition of the *scholarship of integration*, which he defined as "making connections across disciplines, placing the specialties in larger context, illuminating data in a revealing way, often educating non-specialists, too" (p. 18).

The American College Personnel Association (1996), one of the largest student affairs professional organizations, released a document by a group of leaders in higher education and student affairs stating that personal development, student development, and learning were intertwined and inseparable. The document was intended to spark discussion and debate about the role of student affairs professionals in undergraduate education and called on student affairs professionals to "seize the present moment by affirming student learning and personal development as the primary goals of undergraduate education" (p. 5). In fact, it rejected the dichotomy of student affairs and academic affairs as irrelevant to postcollege life and challenged student affairs professionals to strive for a seamless experience for students "by bridging organizational boundaries and forging collaborative partnerships with faculty and others to enhance student learning" (p. 3). This was one of the first publications to explicitly address assessment and the need for student affairs divisions to collect data to document and improve student learning.

The National Association of Student Personnel Administrators (NASPA), joined by the American College Personnel Association (ACPA), another leading student affairs professional organization, followed up in 2004 with

> an argument for the integrated use of all higher education's resources in the education and preparation of the whole student. It is also an introduction to new ways of understanding and supporting learning and development as intertwined, inseparable elements of the student experience. (p. 1)

Separate but strikingly similar conversations occur on the academic affairs front. The AAC&U continues to be an advocate for strong undergraduate liberal education and places integrative learning among it's essential learning outcomes. The Liberal Education and America's Promise project, launched in 2005, investigates the skills college graduates need to be successful in twenty-first-century life and careers (AAC&U, n.d.). The AAC&U draws on data from employers to determine what skills are sought after in the marketplace and details the types of educational experiences that colleges and universities should provide to properly prepare students for the workforce. The AAC&U advocates for a liberal education that results in high-level skills such as communication, problem-solving, and evidence-based reasoning, which students can transfer across contexts.

In the sciences, an emerging field of study called *team science* is structured around the practice of integrating learning across disciplines. Team science is the study of how to bring together experts from different disciplines to solve complex problems (National Research Council, 2015). This type of cross-disciplinary work is at its core integrative.

Despite these parallel conversations in academic affairs and student affairs, a lack of coordination and cooperation among educators remains in these areas in efforts to support students' integration of learning.

Summary

Integration of learning is an essential outcome of higher education. It is the ability to connect, apply, and synthesize knowledge and skills across contexts.

Despite increasing attention toward integrative learning, higher education institutions have not traditionally been organized to promote this type of learning. Instead, administrative and disciplinary boundaries often take precedence and promote a more compartmentalized experience for college students.

Recognition that the division of knowledge into disciplines is an invention of nineteenth-century higher education reinforces the notion of false borders and the importance of crossing those boundaries by integrating learning. Despite the structural evolution of higher education into a compartmentalized organization, undergraduates integrate learning more than most educators realize. In the next chapter, I introduce the integration of learning model, a framework I developed from research with the Wabash National Study and consider the ways that students use connection, application, and synthesis as approaches to make meaning across contexts.

Reflection Questions: Things to Think About in Your Educational Practice

Take a few minutes to read and reflect on the following questions. Jot down your thoughts on paper, your phone, your laptop, or wherever is convenient. Be as formal or informal as you like in how you respond; the important thing is that you give yourself time to reflect.

1. Think about your position in education. Where do you fit on the organizational chart of your institution? What borders exist between you and other educators? Between you and your students?
2. How do you cross boundaries in your work as an educator?
3. Do you see integration of learning in your work? What terms do you and your colleagues use for this kind of learning?
4. Recall Fran's comment about her experience abroad in Brazil and related coursework. Have you had a similar experience of connection?

2
INTEGRATION OF LEARNING MODEL

As educators, we espouse the belief that learning happens everywhere; it's not limited by the walls of a classroom. Learning is happening every day in many contexts, formal and informal, so how do college students connect what they are learning in these different contexts? How can learning from one place bolster learning in another? And how can educators help students to integrate learning better? These are the questions that have captured my attention and my imagination first as a college administrator and later as an educational researcher and faculty member.

When I was a young professional in student affairs administration, I spent a great deal of my time in one-on-one and small-group meetings with undergraduate student leaders. Some of these meetings were with student employees (e.g., resident assistants), and others were with student leaders (e.g., student organization presidents and elected officers). We spent time talking about common leadership and management topics like program planning, accountability, and working with others effectively. In those meetings, students often used what they learned in other contexts to inform their work as a resident assistant or student leader, such as drawing on their experience as a summer camp counselor to think about how to build community in a residence hall or using skills learned in a finance class to help balance a budget as a fraternity treasurer. These connections weren't prompted by me, other than perhaps by my creating the space for students to think. Some students were better at this kind of learning than others, and not everyone did it. I later observed this same kind of integrative learning among college students in the Wabash National Study of Liberal Arts Education (King et al., 2007; Pascarella & Blaich, 2013; Seifert et al., 2010).

In this chapter, I discuss the integration of learning model that I developed in my research and discuss how it is linked to student development, meaning-making, and the college student experience.

The Integration of Learning Model

Based on interviews with hundreds of college students, I developed the integration of learning model as a way to help me understand the *how* of integration. It was clear to me that most students could integrate learning, but I wanted to know more about how they integrated it so that I could help them do so even better. How do students put things together? This question lies at the heart of integration of learning.

I found that students integrate learning in three main ways: connection, application, and synthesis. Students are individuals with their own perspectives and experiences to bring to the learning process, but after listening and analyzing hundreds of conversations with students all over the United States, these three common ways of integrating learning emerged. I think of these three approaches to integrating learning as a pyramid (shown in Figure 2.1) made up of three overlapping triangles: connection and application form the base of the

Figure 2.1. Integration of learning categories.

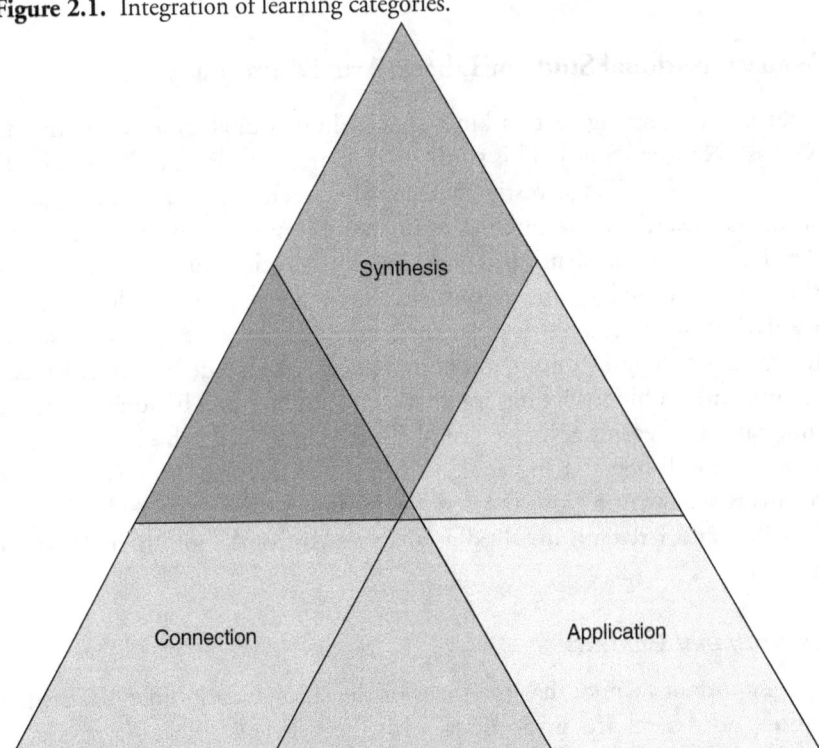

Note. From "Integration of Learning Model: How College Students Integrate Learning," by J. P. Barber, 2014, *New Directions for Higher Education*, 165, pp. 7–17. https://doi.org/10.1002/he.20079. Copyright 2014 by Jossey-Bass. Reprinted with permission.

pyramid, and synthesis is the apex, representing its greater complexity. This illustration characterizes how students use all three approaches in integration of learning, as opposed to a stage-model approach, in an increasingly complex way as the individual advances developmentally.

Later in this chapter, I provide more details on each approach to integration, but first I need to discuss the following things: (a) the national study that guided my work, (b) the developmental underpinnings of learning, and (c) how learning and development are related. These areas will help in understanding how students' approaches to integration evolve over time and explain why first-year students, seniors, and graduate students may have vastly different ways of integrating what they are learning.

Let me explain what the integration of learning model is not. It is not a taxonomy, listing different types of learning akin to Bloom's (1956) taxonomy of learning. It's also not a stage model that assumes a rigid and linear approach to integration; rather, it is a model to conceptualize how people link ideas, skills, and knowledge across contexts.

Wabash National Study of Liberal Arts Education

I set out to investigate this kind of learning through research with the Wabash National Study. This study was a large-scale, longitudinal, mixed-methods project that investigated the ways liberal arts education guided students toward the overarching outcome of wise citizenship; that is, to develop the habits of mind to continually question authority and consider how knowledge comes together to make sense of the world in which we live. Wise citizenship was pursued through the achievement of seven liberal arts outcomes among undergraduate college students: effective reasoning and problem-solving, inclination to inquire and lifelong learning, integration of learning, intercultural effectiveness, leadership, moral character, and well-being (King et al., 2007). I was fortunate to be a member of this research team from the very beginning as pilot data were collected in 2004, and I remain involved as analyses continue more than 15 years later.

Institutional Contexts

It is important to note that the focus of the study was on liberal arts education, not liberal arts institutions, with the belief that liberal arts education and achievement of these seven liberal arts outcomes could occur at a research university or a regional comprehensive institution just as they could at a liberal arts college. In this way, the study was intentionally designed to investigate learning at many types of institutions, and the first cohort to participate in the study included six diverse institutions across the United States. These institutions, with the exception of Wabash College, are identified by pseudonyms:

- Azalea College, a private liberal arts college for women
- Greenleaf College, a private, co-ed liberal arts college
- Golden State University, a public regional comprehensive university
- Hudson College, a private co-ed liberal arts college
- St. Bernadette University, a private Catholic research university
- Wabash College, a private liberal arts college for men

The seven liberal arts outcomes were distilled from the literature related to educational outcomes and linked to quantitative instruments that could measure growth in these areas. As I mentioned in chapter 1, integration of learning was the only liberal arts outcome measured solely with qualitative methods, using an in-depth interview to discover how students were integrating their learning during college. One of the characteristics that makes the Wabash National Study stand out from other research projects is the longitudinal nature of the data collection. Researchers met with students for an interview each year, usually in the fall and usually in person. This data collection from 2005 to 2009 resulted in more than 900 interviews with a cohort of 315 undergraduates (see Table 2.1).

TABLE 2.1
Number of Participants in the Annual Wabash
National Study Longitudinal Interviews

Year	*Interview participants*
Year 1 (2006)	315
Year 2 (2007)	228
Year 3 (2008)	204
Year 4 (2009)	177
Total	924

Note. From Refining King and Baxter Magolda's Model of Intercultural Maturity," by R. J. Perez, W. Shim, P. M. King, & M. B. Baxter Magolda, 2015, *Journal of College Student Development, 56*, p. 763, https://doi.org/10.1353/csd.2015.0085. Copyright 2015 by Johns Hopkins University Press. Reprinted with permission.

Details on the Interviews

The Wabash National Study interview was designed by Baxter Magolda and King (2007, 2012) to examine the practices and conditions that lead to achievement of the seven liberal arts outcomes. In addition, the interviews examined personal development toward self-authorship, a theory of human development explained in more detail in Appendix A. The longitudinal design of the study provided a rare opportunity to revisit the same group of college students year after year to see how their college experience unfolded in real time, an ideal scenario for investigating student development.

The interviews themselves were 60 to 90 minutes long, semi-structured conversations (Baxter Magolda & King, 2007, 2012). When possible, the same interviewer returned to the same campus year after year to interview the same students. A semistructured interview has a number of key topics but is not rigid in the sense that questions must be posed exactly the same way to every student each year. The way the student answered the questions shaped the scope of the interview just as much as the interviewer's prompts; in this way, the students were partners in the research rather than subjects of it. The interviews were audio recorded with the students' permission and later transcribed and shared with the students.

Each interview began with rapport-building and catching up on what happened over the previous year. Students were informed that their responses need not be limited to the formal curriculum and that we were interested in their unique perspectives and experiences during college. The middle and most substantial part of the interview focused on the experiences during the previous year that the students found most significant and how they made meaning of those experiences. Open-ended questions about what the students considered their best and most challenging experiences allowed them to choose the content of the discussion. Each interviewer was trained extensively in interviewing skills, and we probed students to find out not only what happened in students' lives over the previous year but also more important, how they made sense of it. The final part of the interview centered on *integration of learning*, although that term was not specifically used with students. Interviewers asked questions such as, "Thinking back over all the topics we've talked about today, do you see any connections among your experiences?" to prompt students to talk about their process of integration, if they could.

Immediately following each interview, the interviewers recorded a brief 3- to- 5-minute commentary to capture their initial thoughts about the conversation and record any details that may not be clear in the audio file (e.g., emotional responses, context of the interview room, distractions in

TABLE 2.2
10 Positions on the Journey Toward Self-Authorship

Solely External Meaning-Making	
Trusting External Authority (Ea)	Consistently and unquestioningly rely on external sources without recognizing possible shortcomings of this approach.
Tensions With Trusting External Authority (Eb)	Consistently rely on external sources, but experience tensions in doing so, particularly if external sources conflict; look to authorities to resolve conflicts.
Recognizing Shortcomings of Trusting External Authority (Ec)	Continue to rely on external sources but recognize shortcomings of this approach.
Crossroads	
Questioning External Authority [E(I)]	Continue to rely on external sources despite awareness of the need for an internal voice. Realize the dilemma of external meaning-making, yet are unsure how to proceed.
Constructing the Internal Voice (E-I)	Begin to actively work on constructing a new way of making meaning yet "lean back" to earlier external positions.
Listening to the Internal Voice (I-E)	Begin to listen carefully to internal voice, which now edges out external sources. External sources still strong, making it hard to maintain the internal voice consistently.
Cultivating the Internal Voice [I(E)]	Actively work to cultivate the internal voice, which mediates most external sources. Consciously work to not slip back into former tendency to allow others' points of view to subsume own point of view.
Solely Internal (Self-Authoring) Meaning-Making	
Trusting the Internal Voice (Ia)	Trust the internal voice sufficiently to refine beliefs, values, identities, and relationships. Use internal voice to shape reactions and manage external sources.
Building an Internal Foundation (Ib)	Trust internal voice sufficiently to craft commitments into a philosophy of life to guide how to react to external sources.
Securing Internal Commitments (Ic)	Solidify philosophy of life as the core of one's being; living it becomes second nature.

Note. From "Decreasing Authority Dependence During the First Year of College," by M. B. Baxter Magolda, P. M. King, K. B. Taylor, and K. Wakefield, 2012, *Journal of College Student Development, 53*, p. 20. www.press.jhu.edu/journals/subscribe.html. Copyright 2012 by American College Personnel Association. Reprinted with permission.

the interview, etc.). The audio from the interview and the commentary were transcribed verbatim and were the primary sources for analysis. Each student was given the opportunity to review the transcript and provide feedback or corrections, although very few students took advantage of this opportunity.

On a personal note as an interviewer, these meetings were very meaningful. The opportunity to sit down for a 60- to 90-minute conversation with students about their learning is rare, let alone being able to do so each year. Students shared much more about their personal experiences, learning, and struggles than I imagined going into this project. I was also surprised by how easily interviewers and students reconnected during the interviews, even meeting only once per year. I remain surprised by how vividly the interviews that I conducted still stand out in my memory years later. For example, when I reread the transcripts of interviews I conducted, I can recall minute details of the meeting, often including where I was sitting in relation to the student, facial expressions and intonation, and emotions I felt during the conversation.

After each interview was transcribed, a researcher (when possible, the same researcher who conducted the interview) assessed the interview for developmental level in terms of self-authorship. (For more about the systematic process for assessing self-authorship and meaning-making, see Appendix A in this book, and Baxter Magolda & King, 2012.) Each student interview was evaluated for meaning-making using the self-authorship model (see Table 2.2). These assessments gave us insight into how the students thought about information, identity, and relationships, which was very helpful in understanding their approach to learning.

The Link Between Development and Learning

An individual student's meaning-making orientation is important to consider when looking at student learning, and specifically integration of learning, because the way individuals see the world, themselves, and their relationships has a bearing on how they put information together. The integration of learning model I developed aligned very closely with the self-authorship model in the Wabash National Study. That is, students were able to integrate learning more frequently and in more complex ways as they progressed developmentally toward self-authorship. As students became more internally grounded in their meaning-making, the better they could integrate learning.

In the initial phase of my research on integration of learning, I found there was a relationship between the development of self-authorship and the capacity for integration of learning. As students moved toward a more internal framework for meaning-making on the journey toward self-authorship, they also became more adept at integrating learning. As students progressed along the self-authorship continuum, they began to use all three approaches to integration of learning together. That is, as students became more advanced developmentally, they were able to integrate learning more frequently and use different approaches together as needed for the context.

The link between development and learning is clear. A person's developmental level, and by that, I mean complexity in meaning-making, affects the way that person sees knowledge, self, and relationships. Where a person is on the journey toward self-authorship profoundly changes the way they answer these three important questions: How do I know? Who am I? How do I want to construct relationships with others? Meaning-making is complex and fluid over time.

Zaytoun (2005) focused on identity development and the inextricable link between identity and learning:

> Every student has a unique, noteworthy, heartfelt story to tell, regardless of whether his or her experiences emerged from dominant or nondominant identities or both. These experiences create the foundation for each student's capacities for and commitment to learning and engaging in the world. (p. 14)

Who we are is how we learn. Students are not learning clones who are interchangeable in curricular models. Each person is unique and brings their own background characteristics, identities, and lived experiences to the learning process. Our meaning-making, how we see the world, has a direct correlation with how we connect ideas, skills, and knowledge. Who we are is how we integrate.

In thinking about my original question of how students integrate learning across contexts, one can start to see the implications of development on learning. For example, if a college student is early on the developmental continuum and relies heavily on external frameworks and authorities, that student is likely to have trouble connecting learning from two different authorities who may disagree. Conflicting information is difficult to integrate with external meaning-making; it usually comes down to a view that one is right and one is wrong, and therefore the wrong perspective is discarded and not integrated with prior knowledge. However, a student who is further along on the continuum and more developmentally complex would have a different approach to this dilemma. They may encounter the same conflicting information, yet with a more internally driven meaning-making can hold both perspectives in mind at once, weigh them against established criteria and previous experience, and perhaps find a way to reconcile the contradictory points of view. Even though the perspectives are inconsistent, to a more complex thinker they are not automatically incompatible and can be integrated.

This process captured my attention as a new professional and continues to drive my inquiry today. How does meaning get assembled? How do people take disparate information, sometimes in direct conflict, and bring it together in their minds? How do we integrate learning across the multiple contexts we encounter in a single day? And how can educators prepare their students to integrate learning better?

These questions, coupled with my experiences as a student, administrator, teacher, and researcher led to the development of the integration of learning model. In the next section, I describe this model and connect it to the ideas I've discussed about student development, meaning-making, and self-authorship.

Integration of Learning Categories

As an educator and researcher, I am fascinated by how meaning gets assembled, as opposed to how we break down meaning-making into smaller and smaller parts. Dewey (1916) discussed education as the reorganization and reconstruction of experience, and Piaget (1970) envisioned intellectual development as the reorganization and reconstruction of meaning. Perry (1970) shared the value of listening to students and respecting their current ways of meaning-making as a part of the learning process.

As I explained in the beginning of this chapter, I found that students integrated learning in the following main ways: connection, application, and synthesis (see Table 2.3). These categories were originally derived from research on two of the campuses in the Wabash National Study conducted for my dissertation work (Barber, 2009, 2012), and in this book I expand the scope of the data, applying the model across all six of the Wabash National Study campuses, illustrating the principles with examples from students across the country.

Establishing a Connection

Connection, the least complex of the three approaches, is at its heart recognizing similarities. For example, an element of a novel that reminds a student of a television show, or a class assignment that bears similarity to the demands of an internship site. Connections are sometimes superficial and often fleeting but the clear acknowledgment that two elements have a link. To illustrate, Nick, a senior from Greenleaf College described his thinking about his double major in business and philosophy:

I know a lot of people think business and philosophy are polar opposites, just on different ends of the spectrum, but I'm finding a lot of similarities, especially between the upper business classes [and philosophy]. . . . The senior capstone class was very much more philosophical than business-oriented. (Nick, Greenleaf College, Year 4)

Nick recognized some aspects of the subject matter were similar but did not combine these ideas in a way that changed either experience for him. However, he did make explicit the mental and verbal connection that these concepts were related for him.

Application Across Contexts

Application is more complex and involves action: applying information, knowledge, or skills learned in one context to a different context. As such, application is most often hands-on. Many participants in the Wabash National Study talked about writing as first-year students and how they tried

TABLE 2.3
Definitions of Integration of Learning Categories

Category	*Definition*	*Common Student Language*
Establishing a *Connection*	Find a common thread between concepts or experiences that remain distinct; identifying similar elements, foundation, or characteristics.	Compare, compare and contrast, connect, relate, use of analogy, something is like something else
Application Across Contexts	An idea or skill learned in one context is used in a different context; similar conceptually to transfer of learning. Often appears as use of a high school skill or knowledge in college.	Apply, use, transfer
Synthesis of a New Whole	Two or more ideas or skills are brought together to create a new whole; combining knowledge to enhance understanding and gain new insights.	Incorporate, adapt, collaborate, put together, interpret, bounce ideas off one another

Note. From "Integration of Learning: A Grounded Theory Analysis of College Students' Learning," by J. P. Barber, 2012, *American Educational Research Journal, 49*, p. 601. Copyright 2020 by SAGE. Reprinted with permission.

to apply what they learned in high school to writing to the college context. Sometimes this was successful, but other times the five-paragraph essay structure they learned as high school students was not a strong fit for a college research paper; they had to modify what they had learned for the different demands of college. In other instances, students applied skills learned from home to their college activities. For example, Elliot used skills from woodworking with his father growing up to build his fraternity's homecoming float at Wabash:

> Like homecoming, building the float and all that stuff. I've done things like that in the past, so [I] can also go back to my past experiences knowing what I've done in similar situations and [apply] them to the now. (Elliot, Wabash College, Year 1)

Elliot applied skills that he learned as a child in his family context to a student activity in his new collegiate context.

Synthesis of a New Whole

Synthesis is the most complex approach to integration and involves creativity and imagination. With synthesis, a student brings together ideas or knowledge from two or more contexts to form a new way of seeing things. The student synthesizes a new whole from disparate parts. Synthesis was prevalent among more advanced students in the Wabash National Study. As students developed more complex ways of making meaning in terms of self-authorship, they synthesized more often. As the developmental process unfolded over time, I witnessed more synthesis from the participants as seniors than I did when they were first-year students. Synthesis was present for some in the first year, but this approach to integration was much more common in the fourth year. In his sophomore year, Colin talked about synthesis in the context of a religion course, where he took in new ideas, compared the new information with previous knowledge, and then worked to combine the knowledge into a new perspective, distinct from his previous views:

> I take them all in and chew on them and then go to through the digestive process, mentally check it against what I think or thought and how I kind of add this to my ideas and subtract some of the stuff and then combine it all. Kind of getting what I feel is the best of everything. (Colin, Wabash College, Year 2)

These three categories are arranged in order of increasing complexity, and as students became more advanced developmentally, they used all three approaches in concert. This was initially a surprise to me. I fully expected a stage model, where students would master a less complex way of integrating and then move on to a more advanced way of thinking, abandoning the former process. However, the process of integration proved more fluid, with students building on previous ways of integrating and expanding their toolkit of integrative thinking as they progressed through college. It's not necessarily tied to age or year in school, but rather the complexity of a person's meaning-making.

Summary

The integration of learning model that I introduce in this chapter is a tool to help actualize how students put meaning together and consider how we can work with students to facilitate integration even better. Students use three different approaches to integrative learning: connection, application, and synthesis to make meaning of disparate information.

The process of making meaning does not happen overnight. It's a developmental process that unfolds over time and requires reflection, the time to think and rethink. In modern society we don't often give ourselves the time and space to think about what we are learning and how we're making sense of it but doing so can facilitate integration of learning. In the next chapter, I explore the importance of reflection and suggest several ways to build reflection into the college experience.

Reflection Questions: Things to Think About in Your Educational Practice

Take a few minutes to read and reflect on the following questions. Jot down your thoughts on paper, your phone, your laptop, or wherever is convenient. Be as formal or informal as you like in how you respond; the important thing is that you give yourself time to reflect.

1. Think back to a time when things came together for you. What stands out to you about that experience?

2. Referring to the integration of learning model, identify a time in your own learning when you used a connection approach. How about application? Synthesis?
3. How does integration of learning contribute to wise citizenship?
4. Where do you see integration of learning as being relevant in life after college?
5. Consider the student examples from Nick, Elliot, and Colin. How do these students remind you of the students with whom you work? How are their experiences similar and different?

3

REFLECTION

The Foundation of Integration

I am a firm believer that college students do not have enough time to reflect on what they are learning. Too often life in college becomes a series of checkboxes with students' attention focused on the one or two items immediately at hand. After completion of an assignment or task, students quickly move on to the next without taking time to look back on what has been achieved on their list and look ahead at what remains so they can put learning in a larger context. Perhaps it is not just a matter of time. Educators lack training on how to teach students to reflect on what is being learned and how it fits together in the big picture.

Time to reflect is hard to come by, and you often have to build it into your schedule. I love a good ritual, and one strategy for me as a teacher is to do my own reflection. When I ask my students to do a written reflection at the end of most of my classes, I take that time to reflect on my own experience in the class—How did the discussion go? Were there strengths or challenges? What would I adjust for next class and for this session next year? It's not anything formal or eloquent, but it serves the purpose by taking 10 minutes to think, process, and jot down some words in the moment about the experience from my point of view. What I find is that my reflections from those 10 minutes come back to me as I follow up with students during the week, plan class for the next week, and revise my course for the next semester or year. The process of reflecting on my work helps me to be a better educator.

Despite great interest in the practice of reflection, there has been very little consistency over the past century in the definition or implementation of reflection in postsecondary education. Dewey (1933) defined *reflective thinking* as "active, persistent, and careful consideration" (p. 9). Nearly 60 years later, Mezirow (1991) wrote that reflection is the way people transform their meaning perspectives and schemes, leading to transformational learning. I see reflection as an underlying process that enables integration of learning. The act of reflection provides the time and space to process one's experiences, consider how new information fits (or conflicts) with prior knowledge, and undergirds the meaning-making process. Ten years later, Rogers (2001) conducted a concept analysis of reflection in higher education and examined the main terms and philosophical models of reflection. He found four common themes across the models he examined: reflection

> (1) requires active engagement on the part of the individual; (2) is triggered by an unusual or perplexing situation or experience; (3) involves examining one's responses, beliefs, and premises in light of the situation at hand; and (4) results in integration of the new understanding into one's experience. (p. 42)

Reflection is an essential element of all three ways of integrating learning (connection, application, and synthesis), and in this chapter, I examine the ways reflection sets the stage for integrative learning.

A Quiet Mind

We live in a noisy world with constant stimulus from sources physical and virtual. The ubiquitous nature of smartphones, laptops, and other connected devices in the university context means that a steady stream of texts, emails, videos, and social media feeds is coming at college students wherever they go. In this environment, where access to all these forms of media are literally in your pocket, it can be challenging to find time and space to slow down, eliminate the background noise, and think. We need to create opportunities for a quiet mind to reflect, make meaning, and integrate learning.

In considering the role of reflection in learning, it is helpful to return to some of the foundational theories of learning: the concept of general principles by Judd (1908, 1939) and the concept of identical elements by Thorndike (1924). See Appendix A for additional detail on these theories. Tuomi-Gröhn and Engeström (2003) summarized the relationship between Judd's (1908) and Thorndike's (1924) theories of learning in the following:

> The essence of Judd's argument was that transfer occurred because of *what* was transferred, namely principles, and *how* instruction of principles was undertaken, namely, *intentionally, self-consciously,* and *reflectively.* Transfer does not occur effortlessly and mindlessly, as a reflex. The contrast between learning as reflection, and learning as reflex, identifies the fundamental difference between Thorndike and Judd. (p. 21)

Learning is not a reflex occurring mindlessly, and likewise integration is not a reflex. Although we need a quiet mind to reflect, reflection alone does not ensure integration. Simply musing is not enough; action in the form of connection, application, or synthesis is necessary to bring ideas together and, in essence, transform them by way of relating them to one another. Mezirow characterized reflection as an active process of learning that required an astute awareness of the learning process as well as the individual's cognition:

> This rational process of learning within awareness is a metacognitive application of critical thinking that transforms an acquired frame of reference—a mind-set or worldview of orienting assumptions and expectations involving values, beliefs, and concepts—by assessing its epistemic assumptions. This process makes frames of reference more inclusive, discriminating, open, reflective, and emotionally able to change. Frames with these qualities generate beliefs and opinions that will prove more true or justified to guide action. (Dirkx, Mezirow, & Cranton, 2006, p. 124)

This concept of awareness of one's own learning is a crucial link to many of the ideas discussed in this book: self-authorship, metacognition, college experiences, constructivism, and the integration of learning.

Reflection and Metacognition

Mezirow's (1991) theory of transformational learning emphasized that a central role of education is to transform students' perspectives by fostering metacognition, especially how the students' assumptions, biases, and personal characteristics (including background context) shape and "constrain the way they perceive, understand, and feel about their world" (p. 167). Through acknowledging these innate biases and assumptions, students can "change these structures of habitual expectation to make possible a more inclusive, discriminating, and integrating perspective, and, finally, make choices or otherwise act upon these new understandings" (p. 167).

King and Siddiqui (2011) examined the relationship between constructs of metacognition and self-authorship, finding that although both maintain a focus on reflective practice, there are important distinctions. For example, self-authorship acknowledges the role of identity and relationships and positions these aspects of meaning-making as equal to cognition through the representation of the cognitive, intrapersonal, and interpersonal domains. Metacognition gives priority to the cognitive domain with affective elements of identity and interactions and others in the background if mentioned at all. The holistic nature of the self-authorship model adds to the notion of metacognition as reflection by introducing the opportunity to think about one's cognition in relation to, and perhaps as a part of, one's identity and community.

The abilities to be aware of and change habits of mind are central to the foundational theories of learning and development in higher education. Kegan (1994) detailed the shift of subject to object as an indicator of the move from Order 3 to Order 4 (self-authorship) in his orders of consciousness in his model of human development (see Appendix A). Baxter Magolda (1999, 2004b, 2009) examined this subject-object shift in her work on the development of self-authorship. She found that the ability to see multiple perspectives was indicative of growing complexity in meaning-making and necessary for self-authored thinking. I am interested in how people then take these multiple perspectives, sometimes conflicting, and integrate them. Shapiro, Brown, and Astin (2008) stated:

> The capacity to take in new information or adopt new models of reality requires that there be some openness to considering alternative perspectives and viewpoints, recognizing and appreciating that these perspectives are likely to differ from those we've previously held to be true. This requires a willingness and ability to observe our own viewpoints—that is, to not be entirely embedded in or subject to them. (p. 28)

This skill of reflective thought, specifically the ability to hold one's own learning as object and look at it as an outsider, is key to the integration of learning.

Love and Guthrie (1999) illustrated this concept across multiple theories of learning and development, including Perry's (1970) scheme for intellectual development, Baxter Magolda's (1992, 2004a) epistemological reflection, and King and Kitchener's (1994) reflective judgment model. They called this transition "the great accommodation," noting that it happened when a person "comes to realize that uncertainty is neither anomalous nor restricted to certain knowledge domains—that it is evident everywhere. As the place of knowledge, truth, and authority disintegrates, the individual's own role as knower and authority emerges" (p. 79). How, then, can college educators prod students toward this great accommodation? In the next section, I share five activities I have found helpful for individual reflection.

Practices of Reflection

In my work and in my own life, I categorize reflective practices as five activities: thinking, writing, talking, walking, and dreaming.

1. Thinking: Simply take the time to ponder the following: What are you learning? How does it fit with other things you know? What do you think when things conflict? Thinking is likely the activity most associated with reflection: silent and solitary consideration.
2. Writing: Writing is a way of processing your thoughts. This does not need to be formal writing, just a tool to get juices flowing, begin organizing ideas, and capture them to revisit later. It does not even have to be exclusively words, drawing and doodling can be just as effective for processing information. Reflective writing can be private or shared with others. Technology is a powerful tool for written reflection. Tweeting is an example of reflecting with technology (Kassens, 2014), and ePortfolios, social media, and smart wearable devices can all provide prompts for metacognitive awareness.
3. Talking: This means engaging in active conversation or discussion with another person. In this kind of reflection, people share and make meaning with others through verbal exchange. This can be one on one or in a group setting, as long as the conversation happens. The push to speak and respond to another person can be just the right pressure to get a person to put things together in the moment.
4. Walking: Physical activity can be a spark for reflection. I use walking here as a proxy for many physical activities. Walking is my favorite, but physical activity could easily be running, swimming, or biking, which allows the time and space for a person to be reflective. Sometimes putting our physical bodies to work, often in a repetitive or mindless activity, frees up our mind to wander and reflect in different ways.
5. Dreaming: This is unconscious or subconscious reflection. Have you ever experienced waking up with the solution to a problem or an insight about an issue you have been wrestling with? Reflection and cognition do not stop when we close our eyes at the end of the day; often during sleeping and dreaming our minds continue to work through issues even while our bodies are resting.

As we encourage students to make time to reflect, and perhaps create time for them to do so, it is important to remember there is no single right way to reflect. Building reflection into activities that students are already doing is an effective and efficient way to create a habit that will persist through the college years and beyond. Realistic reflection is ideally a mix of all of these actions. Practice makes perfect; with regular practice, we can get better at these forms of reflection.

Meditation and Prayer as Reflection

Meditation and prayer can be productive practices for reflection, incorporating several of the activities previously mentioned. Shapiro et al. (2008) defined *meditation* as an umbrella term that includes a variety of practices such as mindfulness and Zen, with the "common goal of training an individual's attention and awareness so that consciousness becomes more finely attuned to events and experiences in the present" (pp. 6–7). In their review of empirical literature on the effects of meditation related to cognition, Shapiro et al. (2008) documented the benefits of meditation in three key areas relevant to higher education contexts: enhancement of cognitive and academic performance, management of academic-related stress, and holistic student development.

Meditation can enhance a person's ability for metacognition, including awareness of their own cognition, emotion, biases, assumptions, and general ways of knowing. Shapiro, Carlson, Astin, and Freedman (2006) called this practice "reperceiving" (p. 374), akin to Kegan's (1994) notion of a transition from subject to object, achieving the mental capacity to look at one's own thought processes from a less personal perspective outside oneself.

Studies have also found physical evidence of the effects of meditation. For example, Shapiro et al. (2006) noted thicker brain matter in people who meditated regularly. Likewise, Tang et al. (2007) reported that students in China who participated in integrative body-mind training (or simply integrative meditation) showed improvements in attention and self-regulation and lower anxiety, depression, anger, and fatigue.

Prayer is a form of meditation in the context of a religion or theistic tradition. It can be solitary or communal in terms of a prayer group or religious service. Prayer can be formal or informal in structure. Faith-based educational institutions (mainly Christian in the United States) historically included a daily prayer or chapel service, often mandatory, in students' schedules. Although this practice of daily required services is no longer common, faith-based institutions maintain a strong connection to organized religious groups, sometimes at the governance level. Prayer at these institutions may be more visibly included in students' experiences. For example, at St. Bernadette University (a pseudonym for one of the Wabash National Study of Liberal Arts Education's interview institutions) each residence hall has its own chapel where Catholic Mass is celebrated.

Gavin often went to the grotto at St. Bernadette during his first year to pray and reflect on his direction in life. A landmark on the university's campus, the grotto is a smaller scale replica of the original grotto in Lourdes, France, where Roman Catholics believe the Virgin Mary appeared to St. Bernadette in 1858. Gavin said the following in his first interview:

When I . . . turn 40 or 50, . . . what do I want to have accomplished? Do I want a family or, . . . what am I thinking right now, and just kind of recording some of those thoughts in a journal and . . . just trying to . . . figure out some aspects of my life that, you know, I might not have this kind of reflection time moving forward . . . taking . . . quiet and prayerful time to reflect on things. (Gavin, St. Bernadette University, Year 1)

Meditation and prayer are two practices that provide the time to reflect and focus one's attention. In Small and Barber (2019), we advocated for the inclusion of faith, spirituality, and worldviews into the curricula for higher education and student affairs graduate programs. Professionals with career aspirations to work in higher education (broadly in faculty, staff, or administrative roles) need an awareness of the worldviews of their students in terms of faith as well as the faith-based institutional contexts where they may work. In 2018, 31.1% of incoming college students identified as nonreligious or secular (Stolzenberg et al., 2019), and it is important to remember that although the context may be faith based, students' beliefs may differ. These practices of meditation and metacognition are not limited to students who identify as religious.

Structuring Reflection for Students: Reminding, Scheduling, and Responding

Reminding students to reflect is one thing, but scheduling time to reflect is another issue entirely. It means actually making the time for reflection and giving students the space to do it. This notion of scheduling is even better because you are providing the opportunity for reflection and demonstrating its value. We make time in class and meetings for what is most important; incorporating reflection into our work is a clear value statement. One further step is training or instruction on reflection, namely, actually demonstrating how to reflect. For me, this is through a series of prompts (verbal or written) that lead students through a reflective process. I even include the expectation of in-class reflective writing in the course syllabus and respond to students' reflections weekly.

Let's look at how three ways to structure reflection—reminding, scheduling, and responding—can be implemented in practice. Reminding is me saying at the end of class as students are packing up, "We've covered a lot in class today. This would be a good time for you to reflect on what you're learning. Think about that, and I'll see you next time." Scheduling is saying, "We've covered a lot today. Let's take the last 10 minutes of class to write about what you are learning and how it fits with your previous thinking. I have a few questions to guide that reflection today." Responding is offering feedback on the reflection. I could say, "I will collect your written reflections when you're done and offer some brief comments on them. I'd also encourage you to stop by during office hours or schedule an appointment if you want to continue processing these ideas."

This type of guided reflection rarely happens for college students. Students are often left on their own to reflect and process their thoughts. Some are better at this than others, and surely some students reflect and process with peers and parents, but I think that most do not incorporate reflection into daily life. This is truly a missed opportunity in higher education.

Reflection Through Interview Conversations

Many participants in the Wabash National Study (King et al., 2007; Pascarella & Blaich, 2013; Seifert et al., 2010) said they enjoyed the annual interview because it provided an opportunity to reflect in depth on their experiences and learning. Students often integrated learning in vivo during our interviews and told researchers that the conversation served as a much needed space for reflection and connecting learning across contexts.

In this light, I see the act of conversation itself as an intervention that has great potential for promoting learning and development and could be easily recreated through intentional, regular conversations with faculty, staff members, or peers. Academic advising, portfolios, and senior capstone experiences have promise to intentionally promote reflection and integration. Residence life programs are well positioned to foster conversations for students who live on campus with resident assistants, faculty, staff, and administrators. Next, I offer a few examples of the benefits of reflection from students who took part in the Wabash National Study interviews.

Ethan and Kayla

As a sophomore at Hudson College, Ethan commented on the role of reflection in reconsidering one's beliefs. He was an art student who had an insight during his interview that he wanted to reevaluate some of his previous works:

> Yeah, I think I'm going to take more seriously the reflection aspect of progression actually. Because I articulated it in my own head just now. And I just realized as I was talking to you how important it was. . . . I'm probably

going to go back to some of my old projects, into my little archives in my closet [and] take a look at those and see . . . if I can't point out or recognize . . . if there's anything I left out, because . . . I realize about my own self from my writing last year [that] I'll have a different eye now. So . . . I'd actually like to go back and kind of reevaluate a little bit. (Ethan, Hudson College, Year 2)

The Wabash National Study interview itself was a form of reflection; an interview is a context where the promotion of reflection among the participants is intentional. Let's look at Kayla's experience. In her sophomore interview at Hudson College, she expressed one of these moments of discovery promoted by the interview. She discussed how she realized her community service work with an art therapy organization for children was important to her.

In response to the interviewer's questions, "How did you develop these ideas [about community service]? Where did they come from?" Kayla said,

I think this is the first I've . . . articulated whatever I felt. But it's been a thought . . . ever since my Chinese [study abroad] trip. This is the first time I actually put [it] into words. It feels good now. I can tell this to other people (chuckle). It's [interest in art therapy] out now. (Kayla, Hudson College, Year 2)

Kayla had a difficult time responding to the questions, "How did you develop these ideas? Where did they come from?" referring to her ideas about community involvement and outreach. Although she said she had been thinking about these ideas for some time, it was not until she had the opportunity to reflect (in the context of the interview) that she put her ideas into words and linked them to her study abroad experience in China. This example of integration of learning, a synthesis of her academic work and community outreach, is in part a result of the interview itself and Kayla's conversation with the interviewer. As in Ethan's example, his interaction with the interviewer, through a simple conversation about what is important and how a student thinks about college life, created a context for reflection and ultimately integration.

Kayla and Ethan were open to new perspectives. They considered that they might not be right and that there are other ways of seeing the world that were different from their own. The students were confronted with challenges to their previously held beliefs. They both realized, perhaps for the first time, their own capacity for development, or as Ethan put it, "Nothing is ever concrete here [in college,] . . . things are always in a constant state of flux."

Imagine the possibilities for harnessing students' integration of learning if faculty, staff, or other mentors regularly invited students into conversations and guided the discussion away from objective questions such as, "Do you have questions about the material in this class?" to more reflective prompts such as, "How are you thinking about the concepts?" or simply, "Tell me what's important to you about what you're learning." Students might have a difficult time responding to these questions initially, as Kayla did in the preceding comment, but the questions will prompt the reflection that is crucial for integration of learning.

Summary

Reflection is a necessary foundation for integration of learning. Giving ourselves and our students the time and space to reflect on what they are learning is essential for them to then integrate what they are learning. The meaning-making enabled through reflection is key to the practices to prompt integration, which I discuss in the next five chapters. Reflection is the link between the conceptual framework of meaning-making discussed in chapter 2 and the practices that promote integration (mentoring, writing, hands-on, juxtaposition, and diversity and identity) discussed in chapters 4 through 8. Reflection undergirds these practices for promoting integration of learning. In the next chapter, I examine the role of mentoring in integration of learning, including the ways seemingly simple questions and conversations can produce big shifts in connecting, applying, and synthesizing learning.

Reflection Questions: Things to Think About in Your Educational Practice

Take a few minutes to read and reflect on the following questions. Jot down your thoughts on paper, your phone, your laptop, or wherever is convenient. Be as formal or informal as you like in how you respond; the important thing is that you give yourself time to reflect.

1. Can you recall reflecting when you were a college student? If so, what was it like?
2. When was the last time you were intentional about your own reflection as an educator? How can you make time for reflection today?
3. When can you incorporate reflection into your daily routine?

4. Are there certain ways of reflecting (e.g., thinking, writing, talking, etc.) that you favor? Why is this?
5. How do you encourage reflection for your students?
6. How do you schedule and structure reflection for your students? For yourself?
7. What existing student assignments or meetings could be prime spaces for you to add intentional reflection?

PART TWO

HOW YOU CAN HELP:
CREATING EXPERIENCES TO
FACILITATE INTEGRATION OF
LEARNING

PART TWO

HOW YOU CAN USE LEARNING EXPERIENCES TO FACILITATE INTEGRATION OF TRAINING

4

PRACTICE 1

Mentoring Students

There is no replacement for the interaction of individuals. Throughout the Wabash National Study of Liberal Arts Education (King et al., 2007; Pascarella & Blaich, 2013; Seifert et al., 2010), the research team realized that the interview as an intervention had a substantial impact. It was thrilling to see students light up in an interview conversation when asked to talk about what they were learning or what their most significant experiences were. Often, they said, "No one has ever asked me that before!" and then launched into a story, sometimes making meaning and integrating learning on the spot in the interview. Given this response, it was also disconcerting to realize just how many missed opportunities for conversation and mentoring there are in students' college education.

To be sure, there are some compelling examples of mentoring in the Wabash National Study interviews, but what stands out in my memory is the students who lamented the fact that they didn't have a mentor. This demonstrates the absence of mentoring and the missed opportunities, which I think are important takeaways from the interviews overall.

Good Company for the College Journey

Every year in my graduate-level student development class, I assign Baxter Magolda's (2002) article in which she described good company as guidance on a journey. She related this support in terms of three assumptions about environments that promoted self-authorship and three principles of educational practice that lead to personal growth. These six points later evolved into her learning partnerships model (Baxter Magolda & King, 2004).

The three assumptions are knowledge is complex and socially constructed, the self is central to knowledge construction, and authority and expertise are shared in the mutual construction of knowledge among peers. The three corresponding principles of educational practice are validating learners' capacity to know, situating learning in learners' experience, and mutually constructing meaning.

The concept of good company resonates immediately and strongly with most of my graduate students. They read these six tenets and it's as if a magician's secrets were revealed. They can see some of the underlying yet unspoken elements that made them feel good about their own undergraduate learning experiences. For one assignment in my class, students write about who their good company was when they were undergraduates, and these papers reveal strong, meaningful relationships, sometimes more impactful than the mentors themselves may have realized at the time. However, this observation does not align with the findings from the Wabash National Study (e.g., Barber 2019, 2012), where relatively few students discussed strong relationships with faculty and staff as they integrated learning. In most cases, when students described integration of learning, they did it on their own or with the support of their peers.

This difference could be attributed to my course having graduate students versus the undergraduates in the Wabash National Study interviews. It could be that my graduate students are a skewed population; most who choose to pursue a career in higher education have had a positive undergraduate experience. Higher education is largely self-perpetuating in the sense that faculty and administrators often introduce undergraduates to the field through their work. Unless you have college educators in your family, most people do not grow up aspiring to work at a college or university. For student affairs administrators, many can identify the professional who mentored them and showed them that they can do this as a job. Faculty members often identify their undergraduate research supervisor, thesis adviser, or dissertation chair as a the one who encouraged them to pursue faculty work.

Integration of learning is closely aligned with the characteristics of the learning partnerships model (Baxter Magolda & King, 2004) and good company (Baxter Magolda, 2002). The elements of good company and the learning partnerships model capture some of the core ideas on why mentoring is so important for integration of learning. The acknowledgment of the student as a learner, the validation of prior knowledge and experience, and centering identity are all key to integration of learning. What makes the idea of good company special and more than the sum of its parts, namely, the six points in the learning partnerships model described previously (Baxter Magolda & King, 2004), is personal concern and connection. Good company is someone who you know cares about your well-being and success. It goes beyond establishing environments to promote learning and development to interacting and asking the simple but powerful questions, for example How are you doing? What are you learning? How are you putting it all together?

My Undergraduate Good Company

A mentor is a learning partner. A mentor is good company. A mentor is an institutional agent. A mentor is a coconstructor of knowledge. A mentor is an educator. A mentor is a facilitator for meaning-making. Mentors play all of these roles and more.

In my experience as an undergraduate, my key mentor was Ann Leslie Inman. My entrée into higher education and student affairs was through joining a fraternity, and with this experience I gained peer mentors and friends who were involved in campus life as student leaders and employees. I wanted to be like them and work with them. They had a strong community and also relationships with people who worked professionally in the Student Life Office. I was hired as a student employee (work-study) my sophomore year and during that time I realized there was a career path in student affairs. As an adviser when I took on student leadership roles and as a supervisor when I continued working in the Student Life Office throughout my undergraduate years, Ann supported me as an individual and helped me think about higher education as a career, navigating the graduate school application process and eventually finding my way to a master's program.

What was it about this mentoring relationship that sticks with me more than 25 years later? It was Ann taking an interest in me, recognizing my strengths and helping me to hone those skills. It was also acknowledging my weaknesses, and having candid, sometimes difficult, conversations about areas for improvement. It was an ongoing relationship over four years as an undergraduate in which I took on and was given increasing levels of responsibility, sometimes succeeding and sometimes failing, but always feeling supported, and knowing Ann was confident that I could go on to a career in higher education. Over time she also came to know my peer mentors, parents, and other professional mentors in a way that gave her a more comprehensive view of my experience.

This first practice for integration of learning is a bit different from the subsequent four because you're creating a relationship rather than a condition or experience as an educator. It requires an investment of time and effort on the part of the mentor. There are ways to instigate mentoring as an educator without being personally involved, such as including peer mentoring as part of a class or organization or requiring students to find an external mentor. In many cases this practice becomes personal in a way that others do not because it is a partnership that often continues over time.

How is this practice distinct from the others? Well, in some ways a mentor helps process information and make meaning. A mentor then engages in dialogue about those new ideas (i.e., as good company) in making meaning. It's more than just presenting new information and challenging new ways of thinking, it's taking a more active interest in the learning process for a student, the way that Ann did for me.

How Does Mentoring Help Students Integrate Learning?

Previous research on integrative learning has shown that college students do not identify educators as important figures who help them integrate learning (Barber, 2012; Umbach & Wawrzynski, 2005). As an educator, this causes me great concern for the future of higher education. In the Wabash National Study (Barber 2009, 2012) qualitative data, students rarely discussed relationships with faculty members, student affairs staff, or other college educators that played meaningful roles in the integration of learning process. This doesn't mean that educators were absent or not engaged with students, but it does mean that students didn't choose to discuss these interactions. Moreover, college students seemed quite eager for these kinds of mentoring relationships. They don't know they need them, how to ask for them, or even that they can ask for them. But when mentoring relationships happen, they can be powerful.

Many times in the Wabash National Study an interviewer would ask what a student was learning or how they were making sense of something, and the student would think for a minute and say no one had asked that before. In the beginning, members of the research team were worried that students wouldn't feel comfortable talking with researchers they had just met about their college experiences, but students savored these annual interviews, which often lasted over 90 minutes. We found that students enjoyed the opportunity to reflect on and discuss their learning. The attention of a Wabash National Study researcher who was genuinely interested in the student's experience was paramount to the success of these interviews.

Students' lack of reporting influential educators facilitating integration of learning in their college experiences, coupled with their enthusiasm for the interviews, led me to wonder how educators can do a better job of mentoring students and have these important conversations about their learning.

We saw the impact of simple conversations firsthand in conducting the interviews because integration of learning happened in vivo. As we asked students about their learning, they made connections and meaning in the moment. It was so rewarding to see this happen. However, many educators do not have training in facilitating integration of learning or how to mentor students generally (Barber, Bohon, & Everson, 2014).

However, there is hope. Analysis of the quantitative data from the Wabash National Study revealed that high school experiences with faculty mentors, including meeting with high school teachers outside the classroom, had a positive impact on growth in integration of learning over the first year in college (Barber, Barnhardt, & Young, 2017). In data from nearly 5,000 students at 47 campuses across the United States who participated in the quantitative surveys for the Wabash National Study, mentoring experiences in high school made a difference for students' integrative capacity a year later as first-year college students (Barber et al., 2017).

Institutional Agents

An institutional agent is a type of mentor who serves as a guide for students to help them navigate the complex system of higher education. This role is particularly important for marginalized students including first-generation college students, racial minorities, and students from rural areas. Hernández's (2018) research with Latinx students and Sikes's (2018) with rural students demonstrated that institutional agents not only provided vital, practical information about how to get things done at a university (where to go, who to talk to, how to ask, etc.) but also served as mentors, supporting the students personally by building confidence and validating students' experiences.

As students (and indeed as humans), we look to others with more experience than us to show us the way. Where do I start? What do I do next? How do I finish? Am I good enough? Do I belong here? Am I doing this right? Who can help me? How does everything fit together? Some college students struggle to find someone they can ask these sorts of questions.

As college educators, we need to do our best to answer these questions, sometimes without being asked. In my experience with the Wabash National Study, as a student affairs administrator and later as a faculty member, the simplest prompts can open floodgates for students, for example:

- Tell me about what you're learning.
- How do these things relate?
- How do you spend your time?
- What's been your most significant experience?
- Talk to me about your family.
- Who is important to you? Whom are you important to?
- What do you want me to know about you?

Ask one student at least one of these questions once a day, and you will be making a big difference to individual students and big progress toward creating a culture of integration of learning.

The Role of Reflection in Mentoring

Silence is golden. As a teacher in the classroom, I am comfortable with silence. I can ask a question about a reading or an idea and wait patiently for someone to respond. Even if this takes minutes, which can seem like hours, I can be quiet, looking around the room, trying to make eye contact, until eventually someone will become uncomfortable enough to speak up, break the silence, and get the discussion started. This silence doesn't bother me at all because I know it provides necessary reflection time. Sure, some students didn't do the reading or haven't followed the conversation, but most have and they just need a minute to figure out how to put their thoughts together to respond.

    I learned this skill of silence as an interviewer with the Wabash National Study. As a new interviewer, I was afraid of this quiet. I didn't know how to take it. Was it a rejection of my question? Did the student not understand what I was asking? In those early interviews, I would fill this silence with a multiple-choice response. "Tell me about a challenging experience" (No immediate response, then 30 seconds of silence). "Was it a difficult exam? A roommate conflict? Maybe a disappointing grade in a course?" In those moments I took away the students' opportunity to reflect and narrowed their options to three possible challenging experiences. Students usually picked one of the topics from my multiple-choice prompt and continued the interview without a problem, but I inserted myself into their response in a way that I didn't need to. If I had remained quiet, even for 30 more seconds, the students may have come up with a totally different experience to share that they chose and made meaning of.

I soon learned to improve my interview skills through reading transcripts of my interviews and listening to recordings of those interviews. It was sometimes painful to listen to those recordings of my interviews, but it was invaluable to my growth as an interviewer and mentor. I found that the transcripts that contained the most insights from students about their learning and meaning-making had a line or two from the interviewer followed by paragraphs from the student. There were few interruptions and interjections from the interviewer, who was staying quiet to let the students reflect and speak.

This reflection is a normal and necessary part of the integration process as discussed in chapter 3. It is necessary to have the time and space to reflect on ideas to make meaning of them and integrate learning across contexts. As mentors for students, college educators need to ask the questions to get students reflecting and putting things together. It takes time to learn what these questions are for you as they will be different in different professional roles and contexts. A history professor will likely have different prompts to determine integration than a residence hall director. However, once you hone these skills of questioning and quiet, they will become a part of your rapport as an educator and serve you well.

Mentors are confidence builders in terms of integration of learning. They point out the strengths students already possess but may not yet acknowledge, for example, "You have a lot of good experience already, how can you build on that?" "What do you already know that informs this new information?" "You are really skilled in this one area, how can you use your expertise from there over here?" The role of mentors is not to overstep into hyperbole but to remind students that they have valuable prior knowledge, much of it based on their home culture and experiences before college, that can be applied in the university context.

Mentors are also a form of a conscience in integration of learning. They remind students to be true to their values and help them question the way they are putting things together, for example, "Is this change of major the right thing for you? Do you need to pursue a different career path from what your parents want?" Remember, as mentors you are helping to steer the conversation, keeping the student on track as a guide but not the driver.

Differences Among Mentoring, Advising, and Office Hours

Every student needs an advocate, but one educator cannot mentor every student. A single faculty or staff member cannot mentor large numbers of students. If you have a class of 25 students, let alone 100 or 250, you cannot mentor every student, but you can mentor some, you can advise more, and you can have contact with many others. Let me expand on some of these distinctions.

Mentoring is a relationship sustained over time. It implies more than one meeting and may involve several meetings with great regularity. These relationships work best when they are organic and build on some common experience. Blind matching for mentors often fails because it's forced, and there is no natural connection. By contrast, successful mentoring relationships often continue long after the course or even the college career is over.

Advising is not as involved. It implies ongoing attention but may be a step removed from mentoring. Emailing students in an advising group or a seminar is still important for students, but may not be as meaningful as a mentoring relationship. College educators often have a greater capacity to advise students than to mentor students, in part because the contact required for advising is not as time intensive as that of a mentoring relationship.

Office hours are open to all; they may be in person or virtual, and may be a quick conversation that is more business-oriented than personal. It is still an opportunity for educators to make the point to students that they are interested in the students' learning, but it will not immediately rise to the level of mentoring, although a mentor-mentee relationship could evolve from an initial interaction in class or during office hours.

My intention is not to belittle any of these forms of student contact. They all serve a purpose, and a faculty member or student affairs educator could perform all three activities. For example, educators might hold regular office hours in person or online to invite anyone who is a part of their classes or organizations to drop in for a conversation (office hours), directly advise a smaller group of students they have a closer connection with (advising), and form sustained mentor-mentee relationships with just a few students (mentoring).

Benefits for the Mentor

You will find that in these conversations and mentoring relationships you become aware of your own integration of learning. When you ask students how they are putting things together, it's hard not to think about how you're putting things together. These discussions are not only reflective for the students, but also a space for the educator to reflect and integrate learning.

You will grow from these conversations just as the students will. In my view, there is a continuum of mentoring work with students. At one end are professionals who rarely mentor students and actively avoid the kind of emotional work and time that is needed to build a relationship with a student. At the other end of the continuum are professionals who spend too much of their time mentoring and advising students to their own detriment and at the expense of other important work that needs to be done.

Considerations for the Mentor

Although there are great benefits for the student and the mentor when the match is strong, it is not an easy responsibility. Next, I offer a series of questions to consider regarding the details of building a mentoring relationship.

- What level of mentoring and advising can you do well in your role as an educator?
- Are you establishing appropriate professional boundaries on mentoring?
- Does your avoidance of mentoring push those responsibilities to your colleagues? This is a real situation and should be a point of conversation among coworkers (e.g., if you decline to serve on a dissertation committee, does it mean that one of your colleagues will have to?). A candid discussion is necessary about equitable division of time and emotional labor in terms of supporting students.
- What is your referral strategy? If you encounter a student who needs support, but you can't do it, where can you refer them for connection? Our goal should be to always connect students to someone never just leave them with nowhere to turn.
- What are the gender and racial dynamics in mentoring? Are there assumptions, stated or unstated, that mentoring will align along identity lines (e.g., faculty of color supporting students of color)?
- How do we create diverse mentoring experiences and acknowledge limitations? There are pipeline issues in that there are fewer administrators and faculty of color than students of color. It is neither realistic nor fair to assume that every student of color will find good company who is also of color.
- How do we develop and train White faculty and administrators to be good company for students of color?

Mentoring in the Integration of Learning Model

Next, let us examine what this practice of mentoring students looks like for the integration of learning approaches of connection, application, and synthesis. Table 4.1 summarizes the student perspective of the mentoring practice, categorized by an integrative approach (connection, application, and synthesis). The table provides a brief description of what connection, application, and synthesis look like for mentoring. A similar table is provided in each of the next four chapters, one table for each of the five research-based practices that facilitate integration of learning. All five of these tables are combined in Table 9.1 as a comprehensive planning matrix, along with a discussion about creating an integrative curriculum.

Connection

In the mentoring students practice, connection may be a one-time meeting or exchange that lets students know they are not alone. It could be pointing out something the educator and student have in common, like a hometown or a favorite book, or it could be structured with each student scheduling a 15-minute meeting with an instructor or adviser to talk face to face about an assignment. Anything that sends a message that the mentor cares about a student's work and experience and wants to know something about them can serve to bolster connection through mentoring. Connection may be sparked

TABLE 4.1
Mentoring Practice: Student Experiences by Integrative Approach

Practice	Connection	Application	Synthesis
Supporting students through mentoring	Students have a point of contact with a mentor who expresses interest in them and their work.	Students have a mentor who engages in a more in-depth dialogue about how ideas or knowledge from one context are useful in another.	Students have an ongoing relationship with a mentor who helps make meaning about their experiences and helps them see how multiple experiences and knowledge from disparate spheres come together for the students.

by occasional direct messages to students inviting them to meet you in person for office hours, coffee hours (office hours in a local café), or virtually during video chat hours.

Application

In the mentoring students practice, application may be more intentional with targeted questions in a larger conversation, such as "What are you learning in this organization? How are you using these ideas in your classwork? Tell me more about what links you see." In this role, the mentor is facilitating application for the student. For the student, it's that moment of: "No one ever asked me that before." The one-on-one meeting provides the venue and opportunity for students to put their application into words, express it, and perhaps realize it for the first time themselves. To continue building longer term mentoring relationships, end each meeting by scheduling the next meeting time and agreeing on follow-up items that require reflection or action before the next meeting.

Synthesis

In the mentoring students practice, synthesis is facilitated by in-depth conversation that could take the form of long-term planning for a major project, or career. It is usually a series of conversations that keeps returning to the same topics, making progress in meaning-making as you go. These conversations center on how the student is bringing these things together. Synthesis can also link to the development of a worldview: How are students bringing all their knowledge together to make sense of the world? Is it faith based? Secular? How do students reconcile the contrasts they may find between new and old worldviews or others' worldview and their own emerging view? Topics that might not often be discussed are crucial at the point when young adults are developing worldviews and ideal for a longer term mentoring relationship. For me, these conversations are about how the activities I enjoyed as an undergraduate—my fraternity, writing, learning, publication, organizing groups—come together in a career after college. What are the next steps to get to the job, career, and life that you want?

I was mentored as an undergraduate student, and that experience helped shape the direction of my career. Looking back now and using the integration of learning model as a lens, I can clearly see the different approaches to integration at work. I was initially introduced to Ann Inman because of a common connection: fraternity and sorority life. I was a new member of a fraternity eager to learn about this community from Ann, who was a student affairs educator advising the fraternities and sororities. As I moved into more formal roles as a student leader and work-study employee, the mentoring was more strategic and specific. Accountability was also heightened at this point in my experience. When I did something well I was acknowledged, and when I made mistakes there were consequences. As I progressed in my undergraduate career, my experiences as a fraternity member, student leader, and work-study employee were synthesized into a career interest in student affairs administration. Through conversations with Ann and other mentors as an undergraduate, I began to envision a professional path I had not imagined before, a new way forward.

Strategies to Use

How can you help students integrate learning through mentoring? Based on my experiences as an educator and a student, the findings from the Wabash National Study, and the literature related to mentoring in college, I offer several practical strategies for educators to use in their work.

Be Intentionally Selective

Consider how you choose mentees. It is impossible to mentor every student with whom you work. Determine a reasonable number of students to connect with and the appropriate frequency of meetings (one time versus ongoing).

Schedule Interaction

Get it on the calendar. Write meetings on your schedule or plan how you will interact with students. For a small course, it might be a 10- to 15-minute meeting with each student to discuss an assignment or their overall performance in the course; for a student organization, it might be one-on-one meetings with the executive officers. Don't leave it to chance that individual interactions will happen; build them into your plan.

Use Varied Forms of Mentoring

Incorporate different types of mentoring into your experiences for students: peer mentoring (tutors, big brothers), faculty mentoring, adviser mentoring, community mentors, and so on. You do not always have to be the mentor to every student; it would be impossible to do so. However, you can create assignments or expectations for students to make a connection with someone else who can serve as a mentor.

Define the Mentoring Relationship

Set boundaries and clear expectations. For example, meet once a semester for coffee, have a one-on-one meeting every two weeks, or set up a 10-minute check-in during a class session. Whatever the meeting schedule is, be explicit about the boundaries. Expecting a meeting once a month is different from expecting an immediate response to an email over the weekend.

Establish Your Goals for Mentoring Students

Does everyone in the course or group have some experience with mentoring? Perhaps you want to be sure to make contact individually with all students in the first month and then decide to follow up with two or three individuals afterward. Based on those initial interactions, you may be able to connect students with other administrators, faculty, or staff who share common interests or goals.

Finally, Be Realistic

Acknowledge the organic element in mentoring. It's a nice support to assign mentors or make initial contact with a larger group of students as an educator, but it's not realistic to expect every mentoring match to be successful. The point is to help students find the best mentor for them, and it won't always be you.

Summary

In conclusion, simple questions can spark integration. Asking a student, "What are you learning?" or "How does that come together?" can open a door to connection, application, and synthesis. However, too often students are not asked questions like these by college educators. These are missed opportunities for integration of learning that could be initiated with a conversation. Mentoring is a powerful tool for supporting students, making meaning, and creating affinity for a learning environment.

Reflection Questions: Things to Think About in Your Educational Practice

Take a few minutes to read and reflect on the following questions. Jot down your thoughts on paper, your phone, your laptop, or wherever is convenient.

Be as formal or informal as you like in how you respond; the important thing is that you give yourself time to reflect.

1. Who was your first mentor as a college student? Think about what made that mentoring relationship work. If possible, send a note to that person to let them know how being your mentor has affected you.
2. What is your approach to mentoring students? Is it intentional or serendipitous? Is it realistic and sustainable?
3. Do you mentor any students personally? Why or why not? If you do, how did those mentoring relationships begin?
4. Think about multiple ways to introduce mentoring in your work with students. How can you encourage students to identify a mentor to provide them with support?
5. How can you build time for mentoring students into your schedule as an educator?
6. How can students know what to expect from a mentor?
7. How can you teach students what mentoring is and what a mentoring relationship looks like?

5

PRACTICE 2

Writing as Praxis

The idea of writing to promote integration of learning is pervasive in educational practice. Writing plays a key role in the meaning-making process and, as such, is advantageous to students' integration of learning. I think about writing as *praxis*, that is, a regular practice to sharpen a skill. In reframing writing from a form of communication to a daily exercise for better integration of learning, it's reimagined as a way of thinking and learning.

This chapter provides examples of formal writing assignments that encourage students to integrate learning, as well as informal and personal writing activities to dispel the notion that formal academic writing is the only or even the best route. Sample assignments discussed in this chapter include written in-class reflections, capstone projects, portfolios, formal academic papers, digital writing using Twitter, blogging, and journaling along a continuum from private to public.

Teaching writing is one of my great joys as a faculty member. At home and work I get to teach writing across the lifespan by advising graduate students on master's theses and doctoral dissertations, teaching a first-year undergraduate writing course, and helping my own elementary-school-age children with their writing at home. But those are just the formal assignments and activities. Students of all ages are engaged in writing informally all day long: drafting emails, writing social media captions, texting family and friends, and making notes to themselves on sticky notes and in various apps. In my experience, there is an overlap in this process of teaching writing and the practice of mentoring discussed in the previous chapter. Often when teaching writing, I incorporate one-on-one meetings with students to discuss their writing in progress and strategies for improving, which illustrates the relationship between writing and mentoring.

It was overwhelming, although not surprising, to see how much the students in the Wabash National Study of Liberal Arts Education used writing as a tool in their formal and informal educations. Tyler, an African American student at Wabash College, talked about starting a journal in the summer following his first year in college when he remained on campus to work with a faculty member on research:

> I was here on campus working and I just had a lot of time by myself and I started keeping a journal. I think that's probably what did it. . . . I just wrote everything I was too afraid to say or too embarrassed to say and when I started reading back on it [and read] what was I thinking . . . it kind of got the gears going. . . . I think it's good for me because [when] I just write it out . . . I feel better. It's therapeutic. It's catharsis. It's healthy. It's stuff I want to say, but I can't say or it's either stuff that nobody will want to hear about, or nobody will be able to understand . . . my pen and paper . . . listen to me and I'm a happier person. (Tyler, Wabash College, Year 2)

For Tyler, the writing process throughout his college years was strongly connected to journaling, reflection, and thinking about life. In his interviews, it became clear that his identity developed through writing, including his racial identity via processing an incident during his first year in which he was pressured to tell racist jokes at his fraternity for an audience of White fraternity brothers.

Writing is a way of making meaning as well as a way of documenting development. Looking back on past journal writing is in a real sense looking back on a previous version of a person and how they made meaning at that time.

The act of writing is transformative; it helps us make meaning and is a way of organizing ideas, thoughts, and literally integrating our words. Writing helps us put ideas together for ourselves in a medium that allows us to share those ideas with others over distance, time, and culture.

How Does Writing as Praxis Help Students Integrate Learning?

Writing is a way of not only communicating ideas to others but also making meaning for ourselves. Writing can be an important form of reflection, that essential element of integration. The ways writing can help students integrate learning are varied; it can be private (e.g., journal, diary, or notes) to help remember important ideas, record knowledge that doesn't make sense, and generally sort things out on paper or digitally, or it can be public to share ideas across contexts and generations. Public writing can also help integrate learning and has the additional element of feedback from readers. When your writing is public, others may respond to it and agree with you, disagree with you or land somewhere in between.

Writing Across Contexts

Writing is considered a cornerstone of higher education pedagogy. It is not limited to any one discipline or type of institution. Writing is not only a means of facilitating integration of learning but also an intended outcome of a college education. The AAC&U (2009) considers written communication to be one of its essential learning outcomes, alongside integrated learning, and it defined *written communication* as follows: "Written communication involves learning to work in many genres and styles. It can involve working with many different writing technologies, and mixing texts, data, and images. Written communication abilities develop through iterative experiences across the curriculum" (p. 1).

Eodice, Geller, and Lerner (2017) learned that college students found writing projects meaningful when they were able to (a) tap into the power of personal connection; (b) immerse themselves in what they were thinking, writing, and researching; (c) experience what they were writing as applicable and relevant to the real world; and (d) imagine their future selves. These findings clearly tie into the ideas associated with integration of learning.

Likewise, Youngerman (2018) found strong evidence of writing's role in integration of learning and developed a typology of integration in writing through his examination of award-winning student essays at New York University. He found practical strategies that led to connection, application, and synthesis, and noted the importance of writing as a common skill that is valued across virtually all disciplines, even in a highly siloed university. In an analysis of integrative learning in student writing, Youngerman examined two main areas regarding integration of learning and writing: how students integrate learning in writing (i.e., process) and what students integrate in writing (i.e., content). He also found that students used connection, application, and synthesis to integrate learning. His findings aligned closely with my findings from the Wabash National Study (Barber, 2009, 2012, 2014) data. Youngerman also found three forms of content that students integrated in their writing:

> What students integrate can be organized into three broad categories: two sources, multiple sources, and metacognitive sources. When students demonstrate integrative learning by integrating two sources, they often inte-

grate: a text and another text, a text and an art object, or a text and a personal experience. When students integrate multiple sources, it can take the form of: a multifaceted debate, a context, or a set of outside knowledge. Finally, students also demonstrate integrative learning by integrating metacognitive sources either by integrating form and content or integrating evidence of reflective metacognition. (p. 5)

Of particular interest is the notion of evidence of reflective metacognition as this links to reflection as a foundational skill for integration of learning, which I discussed in chapter 3. Reflective metacognition is a complex form of reflection, showing an awareness of one's own cognition and an intention to integrate.

Wallace's Strategy for Writing Papers

Wallace, a student at Hudson College, talked about the challenge of writing academic papers in his first-year and sophomore interviews. The following excerpts illustrate his progression of thought about the writing process. Wallace said that for him, "Writing long papers is really challenging. Once we get over three pages, four pages, I find that's . . . a challenge to me."

In response to the interviewer's question, "How did you make it through it?" he said:

> From a very practical point of view. I defined all of the terms that were in the paper to try to set it up and made an outline [of] what I wanted to talk about in chronological order. . . . You have this problem and there are X many parts to it and eventually all those parts have to add up to . . . prove a point or something at the end. So, I guess that's what I do, I set up a chronological [outline] of how I'm going to slowly persuade people that something's true or something is not true, or whatever. Plus it's just nice to look at a little organized representation [that] makes it seem . . . much more doable . . . the form of the outline has been . . . hammered into my head from high school. I'm not sure if I used it in high school effectively or at all. . . . I never had to write anything over . . . five pages in high school so . . . it wasn't as difficult and it wasn't as introspective. I didn't have to think about what I wrote as much in high school. The outline is much more important to me here, to be able to do long cohesive papers. (Wallace, Hudson College, Year 1)

Wallace's approach to integration in his first year was to apply skills he learned in high school (e.g., creating an outline) to his work in college. Although this met the definition of *integration of learning*, it did not allow any adjustment to his new environment or the expectations for college writing. He simply took the formula learned in high school and applied it to college work. However, a year later, Wallace spoke differently about his strategy for writing:

> You just have [to] write a bunch of stuff down and then I think, I try to make connections and make some sort of interesting thesis type statement. And yeah, I try to realize something about what I read that isn't in any one reading, but when you start to combine them . . . I think it's a lot easier to really be able to think and problem solve when you have a question in front of you, [at least] for me . . . it is. And so I find that by narrowing it like that, I can actually think about it more. . . . And kind of gauge the differences. (Wallace, Hudson College, Year 2)

In response to the interviewer's question, "How do you gauge those differences?" Wallace said,

> Just reading two selections, or something and . . . trying to pick up the subtle somethings . . . I don't know [maybe] create space, where there's something interesting. I'm not really sure. I guess . . . just different accounts of the same thing. (Wallace, Hudson College, Year 2)

In this example, Wallace brought more of himself to the writing process and no longer relied on the formulaic method he applied from high school. As a sophomore, he talked about reflecting on the question, considering multiple readings, and connecting information to find the subtle somethings that would make his paper interesting and alive. Although both comments from Wallace demonstrate integration of learning, his example from his sophomore year is more nuanced and complex. Although it is more nuanced, he approached integration in this example using a simpler approach—connection. This illustrates that although the integration of learning model is ordered from less to more complex—connection, application, and synthesis—it is not intended to be a stage model. Instead, there is a degree of fluidity, and as students become more complex thinkers, they can move back and forth among the approaches to integration and use several different approaches in concert.

The Role of Reflection in Writing

Writing is helpful in integration of learning in two ways: it is a tool for communication, and it is a way of meaning-making. These purposes for writing (communication and meaning-making) are not exclusive; a single piece of writing can achieve both aims at the same time. Sometimes we make meaning for ourselves through writing and then share that writing with others to show them how we made sense of conflicting ideas. Sometimes we make meaning and show it to others to convince them of a certain point of view. Writing allows us to communicate ideas with other people across great distances and across time itself. Writing for communication can be simple or complex; it can be a grocery list to give your partner for an afternoon shopping trip, or it can be a novel that conveys the human experience to people over hundreds of years. Writing for communication is often done for others. We want another person to understand directions, a list, a concept. We want to tell others something about ourselves, our world, our emotions. It is intended to be seen and read.

Writing can also be for making meaning. This kind of writing is more private and sometimes never revealed to another person at all. Writing in this way, perhaps in a journal or free writing on a given prompt, can help us make sense of the world around us. It is a way of sorting things out, gathering our thoughts, and finding out what we value and believe. It is a way of communicating with ourselves. Letizia (2016) wrote about implementing writing as a way of promoting self-authorship and democratic ideals. He developed a three-phase framework for thesis writing that serves to promote personal development. In the first phase (content), the student's thesis uses concrete facts garnered from an authority to make a point. The next phase, evaluation, is inspired by Baxter Magolda's (1999, 2004b, 2009) crossroads phase in the development of self-authorship. In the crossroads, an individual is in transition between reliance on external authorities and establishing an internal foundation for making meaning. Similarly in Letizia's evaluation phase, the student's thesis is an evaluation and interpretation of facts rather than merely a statement of facts. Finally, in the third phase (ownership or creation), the student's thesis is original, at least to the student, akin to entering self-authorship in Kegan's (1994) and Baxter Magolda's work. In writing to create meaning, we can try out different ideas, identities, and ways of integrating before sharing them with others.

In all these configurations, writing is a powerful tool for integration of learning because it forces us to slow down and put our thoughts into written words either using a keyboard or pen and paper. Writing is a luxury that many rarely allow themselves; it is the chance to reflect, think, process, edit, and revise.

College students today are writing constantly. In addition to the writing in the formal curriculum, such as research papers, journal entries, or case studies, students are constantly texting, commenting on social media, and jotting down notes on smartphones. Technology has not reduced writing, it has increased it. Writing is not all formal prose, there are different forms of writing, but it is written communication all the same. Educators need to help students see the connection among various forms of writing and teach them how to translate the information, emotions, and humor that is conveyed easily through digital media to the more formal writing often centered in college courses.

Portfolios in Action

Electronic portfolios are excellent tools to use the impact of writing for integration. (Portfolios are described briefly here and discussed in greater detail in chapter 10.) Portfolios allow students to curate their writing projects, along with other work, to document their learning and tell the story of their learning. Portfolios use writing on the following levels: (a) to showcase formal writing created in the context of students' courses (research papers, essays, fictional work, etc.) and (b) framing writing, the reflective and organizational writing that serves as the framework and road map to the portfolio (Eynon & Gambino, 2017; Reynolds & Patton, 2014).

Another strength of an electronic portfolio is its ability to show how writing, meaning-making, and learning change over time. Have you ever returned to old journals to reread previous thoughts? It is sometimes uncomfortable to see your earlier ways of writing and thinking, but it also clearly shows how far you have come.

This is a process with which tenure-track faculty are familiar because of the promotion and tenure process. It is necessary to submit samples of published writing like journal articles, books, and chapters to illustrate your scholarship and the public scope of your work. It is also necessary to write the framing language that puts these writing samples in context. How do they come together into a cohesive research agenda? How is your scholarship related to your teaching? The tenure dossier is in a sense a portfolio of your work as a faculty member.

Writing Experiences in the Integration of Learning Model

Next, let's explore how writing experiences facilitate the three approaches to integration of learning (connection, application, and synthesis; see Table 5.1). These characteristics, along with those from the other four practices

TABLE 5.1
Writing Practice: Student Experiences by the Integrative Approach

Practice	*Connection*	*Application*	*Synthesis*
Writing	Students explore through writing as they search for similarities in ideas. Writing is a process to search for relationships.	Students use writing formulas or a framework learned in one context and apply it in another context. At first, this can look like mimicking another author's work. It is hoped that somewhere between plagiarism and making it one's own, there is a place for modeling and imitation: "This is how to do it."	Students bring together disparate ideas into a new written narrative that didn't exist before. This is a creative process, sometimes abstract in nature.

described in this book, are compiled into a planning matrix in chapter 9 to help you consider how to use them in concert to form an integrative curriculum.

Connection

In the writing practice, connection may look like free writing or a simple acknowledgment of similar ideas. It could be more experimental, with free writing as a method of trying to uncover links. Journaling fits here as sometimes connections are discovered through the writing process. It could also be simple notes and word associations. For example, morning pages, popularized by Cameron (1992), is a practice designed to freely make connections by writing three pages of stream-of-consciousness thoughts in long hand immediately on waking up.

Application

Application in the writing practice may look somewhat formulaic; for example, the student applies a framework learned in one context to another context. It doesn't have to be successful. A common example in the Wabash National Study was from first-year students, who tried to use a writing formula (e.g., the five-paragraph essay) from high school for their college writing. It was definitely application, but students soon realized that their high school formula did not meet the expectations of college-level writing. In Youngerman's (2018) investigation of student writing, he found that when students integrated learning by application, it took the form of one author's language being brought to another author or the realm of ideas or art objects being tested in or exported to the everyday world.

Synthesis

In the writing practice, synthesis is a creative process in which a student brings together disparate ideas into a new narrative. This could be an abstract exercise such as combining lived experiences from home life with a new setting to create fiction, merging theories from two different disciplinary fields to create a new framework in academic writing, or bringing two or more cultural traditions together through writing, perhaps in multiple languages. This might also be creative in the sense of fiction writing, that is, combining lived experiences and what one knows with fiction and fantasy to bring to life a new story through writing. Remember the full title of this category is Synthesis of a New Whole (see chapter 2, p. 34, this volume). Youngerman's study revealed that students integrated learning in writing using synthesis through the process of generating an idea, forming a judgment, following an implication, or gathering sources.

Let's return to Tyler's comments for a moment. His writing progressed as he continued his college education, and by his senior year, he considered himself to be a much better writer. In his fourth and final interview for the Wabash National Study, he described the process of preparing a writing sample for graduate school applications. He shared his draft with faculty members at Wabash College and received constructive feedback on how to improve his writing. Tyler talked about the feedback and revision for his writing in his fourth year:

> I need [critical feedback] and it's really healthy. It keeps me humble and it keeps my head on straight. It keeps me working and makes my writing better and whatever I'm producing better. So I like getting it, but it's still, nonetheless, difficult to digest sometimes. I can rewrite . . . 30 times and at some point you just want it to be done and you want to hear them say this is it. This is [a] good product. You can move on. (Tyler, Wabash College, Year 4)

In response to the interviewer's question, "And have you gotten to that point yet?" Tyler said, "Still working on it."

Tyler used synthesis in this example, combining his original drafts with feedback from his mentors to create something new. He saw revision as a healthy and necessary part of the writing process.

Strategies to Use

Based on research findings from the Wabash National Study and the literature on writing in the college context, I offer a number of strategies for educators to implement in facilitating integration of learning.

Journals

Writing in a journal may be a private form of writing or shared with select others. It is generally a safe place for writing one's thoughts, fears, questions, and concerns and a process for documenting one's day-to-day activities and interactions. Regular journaling is a series of writing episodes, crossing periods of time in the writer's life. A journal can be a place to track the evolution of ideas and integration of those ideas over time. Rereading past writing in a journal can be an important part of integration by reviewing past perspectives to consider how one's thinking has changed and ponder how ideas have been integrated across contexts.

Faculty members might assign students to keep a reading or observation journal to record ideas, questions, and notes about what they are learning. The same strategy can be useful for student affairs educators working with student leaders; keeping a journal about leadership roles, group dynamics, or other skills learned in cocurriucular activities is an excellent way to document learning outside the classroom. The format and assessment of journals can vary widely. Journals can be shared with the educator but don't necessarily have to be graded or evaluated. Alternatively, you could ask students to share some of their insights aloud to the larger group if they are comfortable doing so. In any case, it is important to set the expectations for privacy up front to build trust with students so they know what to expect.

Written Reflection and Free Writing

As mentioned previously in this book, giving students the time and space to reflect is crucial for promoting integration. For faculty members, devoting time in class or during a student meeting for written reflection ensures that students engage in this activity. If assigned as homework or something to do on students' own time, the reflection often doesn't happen, or it does but with distractions. (To be honest, this is something many people, myself included, struggle with, not just students.)

Once you reserve time for reflective writing, there are several formats you can employ. Structured reflection, semistructured (with guides or prompts), and unstructured free writing are all possibilities. The prompt could be simple such as, "We've covered a lot in the past week. How are you putting everything together?" There is no right or wrong answer; what's important is the opportunity to reflect and allow space through writing to connect, apply, and synthesize. In my practice, I do not grade the content or format of the written reflection, I only respond with comments and observations. If a student introduces a factual error or misunderstanding in the reflection, I point it out in my comments, but I do not correct spelling; grammar; or, since the intention is to write freely and focus on the flow of ideas, the mechanics of writing.

In my teaching, I reserve 10 to 15 minutes at the end of each class for students to participate in a written reflection. I provide an open-ended prompt related to the topics we have studied that week and collect the responses from students before they leave class. I encourage students to write the reflections by hand rather than typing them out. This practice serves the following purposes: (a) It gives students dedicated time to get their thoughts down on paper before they return to their busy lives; (b) it gives me immediate feedback on my teaching and facilitation because, from reading the students' reflections, I can get a sense of what students took away from the class and where I need to clarify understanding; and (c) it gives me a natural starting point for the next class. I hand back the reflections with my comments at the beginning of the following class and explicitly link what we discussed in the previous meeting to what we're studying next.

Tweeting

Tweeting is a public form of writing on a platform that promotes a stream-of-consciousness approach that allows people to create meaning in the moment. For a short post, 280 characters is all that's allowed, this is doable for students and not overwhelming. It also can't be edited (at this point) so there is a sense of forgivenesss in terms of spelling. A post doesn't have to be perfect. The thread format of replying to one's own tweets to write a longer narrative is a helpful structure in that it promotes a logical progression of ideas. After the first point, follow that up with the next point, and the next, and so on. In following a thread, you can often see the person making meaning and integrating in real time.

Similar to my use of written reflections, I use Twitter in one of my classes (Assessment and Evaluation of College Student Learning) as a way to capture student understanding at the end of each class period. Each student creates a Twitter account as part of the class, and I end each session with the simple question, "What did you learn today?" Students tweet at least one response before they leave, and some tweet more than one thing they learned. Because Twitter is a public platform, the whole class (and the whole world) can see each other's responses by following the class hashtag (#EPPL525). Occasionally former students of the course, faculty colleagues, or book authors who are mentioned in the tweets will respond and join the conversation. As students become more comfortable with the platform, they reply to one another and share pictures from their notes, readings, or class assignments. Some students also continue conversations about class topics on Twitter after class and throughout the week. This activity gives me an immediate read on what students see as the main takeaways of each class session, and it often reveals that students' main takeaways are that differ from mine. I can then begin the next class by clarifying any information and reemphasizing important points I think may have been overlooked.

Blogging

Blogging is another public mode of writing that can promote integration of learning for students. How is this different from Twitter? It's a longer form and more readily allows the inclusion of different forms of media—photographs, videos, audio files, websites, and so on, without the limitation of 280 characters. Blogging also builds on itself, so with regular blogging you have not only a collection of several posts but also an ongoing narrative and record of the evolution of your thinking over time.

Mind Mapping

Mind mapping is a form of nonnarrative writing to help visualize relationships among ideas. The process of writing is a part of mind mapping, but it is usually not in the form of complete sentences or paragraphs. The focus is creating a visual representation (map) of how different ideas are connected. This is a way to map integration and actually show with lines, arrows, or shapes how ideas, knowledge, and skills are related and in proximity to one another.

Word Association

This is a simple activity that is exactly what it sounds like. The facilitator introduces a word, and students write down the first thing that comes to mind. This initial reaction might be followed up with a few minutes or more of deliberate reflection and writing to help the students explore the connection between the two ideas—the educator's prompt and their initial association.

Workshopping

This is a favorite practice of mine from my time as an undergraduate English major. In this exercise, students share a draft of writing in progress with a small group of peers. The peers read the work (this may happen in advance) and then provide face-to-face feedback on the writing. Participants must practice collaboration, constructive critique, and vulnerability in the process. Workshopping is a way of developing or moving the writing forward and at the same time integrating the original draft with the workshopping feedback to produce a new, revised draft.

Writing Conferences

This practice is a combination of writing and mentoring. The instructor schedules 10- to 15-minute meetings with individual students to discuss their writing in progress. When I hold such conferences, I ask students to submit a draft of their work in advance, and I read and make comments on the paper ahead of the conference. When we meet, I ask the students what they think they did well in the draft and what they found challenging about it. Then I walk through their strengths and my suggestions for improvement from my comments (only the big ideas, not reviewing every detail). I end by asking the students what questions they have for me and how I can help them with their next draft. These conferences are more personal than just returning a graded draft with comments, and also ensures that students hear the feedback from me rather than skipping ahead and going directly to the final grade.

Summary

Writing is an important part of daily life for college students and spans formats from formal research papers for academic credit to informal text messages to friends and family. Writing can be for private reflection, public consumption, or a blend of the two. Among the practices for promoting integration of learning, writing stands out as a means for prompting integration of learning as well as a documentation of integrative learning. In the next chapter, I examine the ways juxtaposition—placing two seemingly unrelated, disparate, or conflicting ideas together—can advance integration for students.

Reflection Questions: Things to Think About in Your Educational Practice

Take a few minutes to read and reflect on the following questions. Jot down your thoughts on paper, your phone, your laptop, or wherever is convenient. Be as formal or informal as you like in how you respond; the important thing is that you give yourself time to reflect.

1. What is your first memory of writing?
2. As a college student, what forms of writing came naturally to you? Which were more difficult?
3. What formal and informal writing can you incorporate into your work with students?
4. How much in-class or in-meeting time can you reserve for students to write?
5. How much time can you reserve for yourself to write or make journal entries for yourself?
6. How do you pass on your beliefs about writing to students, either intentionally or unintentionally?
7. What forms of writing do you think your students gravitate toward? How do these compare with the forms of writing you value?
8. What forms of writing are you biased toward or against? Why?

6

PRACTICE 3

Encourage Juxtaposition

Experiences that deliberately encourage the juxtaposition of different perspectives promote integration of learning for students. Group discussions were a frequent example in the Wabash National Study of Liberal Arts Education interviews, particularly when an educator or adviser served as a facilitator, bringing diverse participants into the discussion and introducing new, and sometimes conflicting, information into the conversation. Intentionally including diverse perspectives in contributions from texts, films, and panelists in an educational experience provides an opportunity for students to wrestle with dissonance and decide how conflicts can be reconciled, if at all. The experiences discussed in this chapter include problem-based learning, decision-making, facilitating diverse group discussions, and developing reading and video lists.

Class discussions are a common pedagogical tool and an opportunity for an educator to challenge students to look at issues from different perspectives. Matt, a sophomore at Wabash College, described an experience with one of his professors that taught him to examine multiple perspectives on topics that may be controversial and not often discussed in academic coursework:

> He's probably one of the best professors that I've had as far as making me think because we would have a bunch of really in-depth discussions . . . about different things that you would be afraid to speak up with. I mean we're talking about Jewish upbringing and why there's so much anti-Semitism and all these different things. . . . We had a speaker . . . who's a former UN representative who did his thesis on trying to go over the border from Mexico into the U.S. and wrote a book on it. It was just far different than what you see on television and you get to know that . . . there's always

two sides and if you don't get both sides you can't have a balanced view....
[I used to have these headlines in my head] of people sneaking across the
border, building tunnels, jumping fences, and you don't get to hear about
how just sneaking across the border for one day is enough money for them
to feed their families for a month. The different motivations on why they
[immigrants] do it [come over the border into the United States illegally].
I just think it [Multicultural Literature class] gave me another tool to be
able to be level-headed about a vast spectrum of things. I know there's a lot
of people that push out subjects and will talk about immigration or something and not really know exactly both sides of it and just be real quick to
judge and have their mind set on a position, and now I feel obligated to
present them the other side. (Matt, Wabash College, Year 2)

For Matt, putting together the two contrasting ideas of media coverage of issues at the U.S. border with Mexico and a guest speaker's research on the topic prompted him to integrate learning. His experience with small-group discussions in a multicultural literature class helped him gain confidence introducing his own ideas and learn how to integrate them with other peoples' perhaps opposing ideas

Juxtaposition can be an effective means for encouraging cognitive dissonance. It is necessary to bring different, sometimes conflicting, ideas together for students to wrestle with. This wrestling process can be challenging, but it's where some of the most significant integration happens. Students are forced to consider alternative points of view, figure out if conflicts can be resolved and if so how, and ultimately integrate new perspectives with previous experience.

Restorative justice initiatives on campuses are a practical example of juxtaposition in action (Lipka, 2009). Many institutions are moving from a judicial and punitive approach of handling student misconduct to a model of restorative justice that encourages students to consider the impact of their actions on others and understand the perspectives of those who have been affected or victimized as a result of misconduct (Schrage & Giacomini, 2009). Placing these perspectives of offenders and victims together challenges students to make connections, and consider how two or more sides of the story intertwine.

A skilled educator can play devil's advocate in a discussion or activity, introducing readings, examples, or exercises that push students to consider new ideas and challenge their existing ways of thinking. The key is to place disparate things together to encourage students to compare, contrast, and ultimately integrate learning. How are these things similar or different? Comparing and contrasting might initially lead to a connection, but figuring out how they can be reconciled may lead to synthesis eventually.

How Does Encouraging Juxtaposition Help Students Integrate Learning?

Class discussions, particularly in small seminar-style groups, were strong examples of juxtaposition in the Wabash National Study. Study abroad trips were also examples because they often placed a U.S. student's American or Western lens in juxtaposition with a different cultural lens. This juxtaposition was more extreme the more divergent the cultures were. For example, a U.S. student visiting China experienced differences in the spoken language, written language, food, currency, and economic and political systems. A U.S. student studying abroad in the United Kingdom or Australia experienced some juxtaposition but not as much.

When we put two items or ideas side by side, our instinct is to compare them and try to find a connection. For example, apples and oranges are different colors and have different textures. A thick peel covers an orange, and an apple has a thin skin. But they're both fruit grown on trees and are both edible. I might not generate this list of similarities and differences if I did not see an apple and orange side by side or have someone prompt me to think about these two items together, but the act of putting them next to each other sets in motion a cognitive process to try to relate them to one another.

One aspect of juxtaposition is compare and contrast, which I see as a precursor to integration of learning. Comparing and contrasting is not integration; rather, it's holding up two separate ideas or concepts and measuring them against one another. This might lead to a connection but not necessarily if the student is only acknowledging the differences and is unable or unwilling to contemplate how they relate to one another. For example, a student might say, "Here is an apple and here is an orange. Let me tell you about each one and how they're different." If students are not connecting, applying, or synthesizing in this presentation they are not integrating. Therefore, educator involvement in actively promoting and facilitating integration of learning is essential. Simply putting two disparate ideas or perspectives side by side does not ensure students will integrate them. It takes skill, patience, and sometimes strategy to help students cross that bridge from comparison to integration.

Aggregative Versus Integrative Approaches

The National Academies of Sciences, Engineering, and Medicine (2018) described this phenomenon using the faculty perspective, noting that faculty training is often so specialized that it becomes an obstacle to integration:

> In an environment in which faculty tend to be trained by, and squarely located within, a discipline (and corresponding department), efforts at achieving interdisciplinarity in research and education are difficult, and are initially more likely to be aggregative than integrative; that is, they will tend to draw dollops of material from the various different pools of disciplinary expertise in parallel rather than bring them into conversation or productive confrontation. (p. 99)

This difference between an aggregative approach and an integrative approach is crucial. An aggregative approach places the onus of integration on students by presenting juxtaposed information to them but stopping short of guiding them into integration. In this model, it is assumed that students will see the links in the knowledge that is presented and integrate it on their own. Faculty members are limited by their own disciplinary focus and do not (or cannot) help them to do so. Sometimes integration of learning does happen on its own, but often it's a missed opportunity.

Higher education thrives on juxtaposition. However, the approach is too often aggregative rather than integrative. We put ideas, skills, and experiences close to one another all the time and hope that students can integrate them on their own. Courses are discrete 3- or 4-credit bundles that make up a 120-credit undergraduate degree. Some of those courses directly connect to one another through prerequisite requirements or the sequencing of a major, but most are positioned next to other courses either concurrently in the same semester or in adjacent semesters without regard to the topics or faculty. General education requirements are juxtaposed with major requirements.

Students participate in cocurricular activities like athletics, intramurals, organizations, and leadership programs alongside curricular requirements. Some areas, like intercollegiate athletics, have strongly coupled experiences that help support student academic success and have dedicated staff and resources. Other cocurricular experiences support the academic lives of students but offer limited resources to help integrate learning. Work experiences are also juxtaposed with the curriculum, sometimes by design, in the form of credit-bearing internships, and sometimes out of necessity, as illustrated by the 70% of college students who work at least part-time during the academic year (Carnevale et al., 2015).

Juxtaposition is also a common strategy in residential programs. Some of the earliest institutions, such as Oxford and Cambridge in the United Kingdom, brought together faculty, students, classroom space, dining halls, and living areas under one roof. Universities in the United States recreate this configuration with residential colleges, faculty in residence, and classroom spaces in residence halls. These common elements of living learning communities bring together different ideas and put them next to each other, encouraging students to integrate.

Finally, in building a diverse campus community, we are actively juxtaposing people from different backgrounds. As I discuss in chapter 8, structural diversity matters on a college campus; bringing together students, faculty, and staff with diverse identities and histories puts different ideas, customs, languages, and traditions next to one another. When different ideas, cultures, languages, and epistemologies interact, the environment is conducive to reflection, dissonance, juxtaposition, and integration.

The Role of Reflection in Juxtaposition

As detailed in chapter 3, reflection is the foundation of integration of learning. In this section, I dive into how reflection relates to juxtaposition and ultimately integration of learning. Putting different ideas side by side and considering them together can be awkward or even painful. Festinger's (1957) theory of cognitive dissonance has two main tenets:

1. When a person is in a state of dissonance, which is the position of being psychologically uncomfortable, they will try to reduce that feeling and achieve consonance, which is a position of agreement or consistency.
2. When a person is in a state of dissonance, in addition to trying to reduce it, they will actively avoid other situations, knowledge, and contexts that add to the dissonance.

In a university or college environment when students encounter something that does not line up with what they know, they may try to resolve that psychological discomfort through either rejection and avoidance or connection, application, and synthesis. If a student is in a situation of trying to resolve dissonance, they will avoid scenarios that may add fuel to the fire of dissonance until the inconsistency is resolved. Taken together, Festinger's hypotheses suggest that cognitive dissonance can be a driver of integration of learning as well as a deterrent.

How students respond to juxtaposition is mediated by their level of meaning-making. A student who is reliant on external frameworks may encounter two juxtaposed statements that conflict, or cause psychologically uncomfortable moments and may seek a trusted authority figure such as a parent, teacher, or supervisor to ask which one is correct. This may not lead to integration of learning at all; the student may accept the authority's response without question and move forward. Dissonance resolved. However, students who are at the crossroads of their self-authorship journey might struggle a bit more, seek advice from trusted authorities. and also wrestle with how to resolve the dissonance themselves. An educator with an eye for integration can push students toward that second scenario by prompting them to struggle with the dissonance longer rather than providing a quick resolution to the dissonance. The danger is in the second tenet of Festinger's (1957) theory, or when people are in a state of dissonance they will actively avoid new information that will contribute to the dissonance. This could result in the student shutting down in a class or program or staying away entirely.

As educators, this middle ground is where we strive to be, providing enough cognitive dissonance that students are psychologically uncomfortable and try to resolve it preferably through a process of integrating learning. At the same time, we keep students engaged and support them so they do not retreat from the situation completely. We may juxtapose ideas intentionally to prompt thought, discussion, and ultimately integration, but we also must be present to support students through that dissonance and provide tools for integration of learning.

Juxtaposition Experiences in the Integration of Learning Model

Next, let us examine how the three approaches to integration of learning (connection, application, and synthesis) appear in juxtaposition (see Table 6.1). As a reminder, chapter 9 features a table combining characteristics of all five research-based practices to facilitate integration of learning as a comprehensive planning matrix.

TABLE 6.1
Juxtaposition Practice: Student Experience by Integrative Approach

Practice	Connection	Application	Synthesis
Juxtaposition	Students compare and contrast ideas that are placed next to one another; they recognize interesting or disconcerting differences.	Students actively wrestle with how disparate, perhaps conflicting, ideas can coexist.	Students find ways to reconcile juxtaposed ideas into a new way of seeing the knowledge and perhaps the world.

Connection

In the juxtaposition practice, connection may start with compare and contrast or, even more simply, an acknowledgment that there are disparate ideas, but for integration, the individual must go further to relate the ideas or skills. A student may realize there is a similarity between two concepts but may not be able to figure out how they relate to one another. Connection is more about the establishment of a relationship than determining what the relationship actually is. In this category, a student may simply acknowledge that two or more things exist in the same space, and they are interesting together.

Sydney, a sophomore at Greenleaf College, recalled finding connections in the juxtaposed courses of her first-year college curriculum:

> You make connections, different ideas . . . all classes [sort of] relate to each other, but it's not until you make those . . . leaps. [For example,] we talked about Africa in my English class. . . . It's just funny, how you make those connections from different things . . . I mean psych and child development are kind of the same. But you just talk about . . . different aspects of things and they just make connections. So, that's how I see it . . . related [back] to friends. You . . . find out stuff about people, and . . you feel . . . closer to them, and . . . if you're connected to someone, you're able . . . to talk to them, you're able to relate to them. . . . I would say [you would] have a better time with that person. . . . [In high school] everything was . . . sectioned off. And I feel like when you take a class at college, you're learning about life. You're not just learning about that topic, you're learning about how that relates to everything else that's happening in the world. (Sydney, Greenleaf College, Year 2)

Sydney began to see her curriculum as more than simply a series of individual courses that happened to take place in the same semester. She recognized relationships and made connections among them; she also noted the divergence from her high school curriculum in which courses were still juxtaposed in a similar way but she saw as being "sectioned off."

Application

In the juxtaposition practice, application may look like a struggle to put a puzzle together. The student realizes that two ideas or elements of knowledge are related but actively struggles to figure out how they fit together. The key in application is that a student is doing something. In connection the focus is on recognition of a link, but application is holding up those puzzle pieces, turning them around to see how they might fit together (sometimes like trying to put a square peg in a round hole), and really trying to figure it out. Perhaps this involves using (applying) a lens or conceptual framework from one class or setting to help understand conflicting ideas in a different context.

Synthesis

In the juxtaposition practice, synthesis may look like finding a way to bring together the juxtaposed ideas into a new form. It could be a fairly simple compromise such as taking equal elements from each idea and incorporating them, but it is not a formulaic average. It could be more complex in the sense of weaving strands of multiple ideas in a way that is truly unexpected and looks different from any of the original ideas. The important concept of synthesis is bringing knowledge in a creative process to form something new that did not exist in any of the original ideas. It is a new whole, a new way of seeing things.

The role of integration in the process of cognitive dissonance is not to find an average or a happy medium. It is to reduce the dissonance, not eliminate it, and connect, apply, and synthesize knowledge to better understand the world. For example, if two juxtaposed statements that arouse cognitive dissonance are "the Earth is round, and the Earth is flat," the resolution through integration is not "the Earth is slightly curved." For example, a student using a synthesis approach to integration might reason in this way:

> The Earth looks flat to me and that's what I have always assumed it to be. But the textbook and my teacher tell me that the Earth is round. How can I put those together? The Earth is so large that I can't see the shape from where I stand. It looks flat to me in my little section of the planet, but if I looked at the Earth from the Moon, I would see that it is actually round.

This line of thinking brings together two ideas to form a new way of understanding things. In human learning and development, there is no formula for integration or reducing cognitive dissonance. It takes work, reflection, and time.

Students with less complex meaning-making will be unable to have multiple perspectives simultaneously. The ability to see multiple perspectives is characteristic of students entering the crossroads of Baxter Magolda's (2009) self-authorship theory or multiplicity in Perry's (1970) theory of cognitive development. Before that point in development, students look for an authority to give the right or the best answer and then believe and defend that one perspective against all challengers. Juxtaposing contrasting ideas to this student will result in the wrong idea being swatted away in favor of the authority's right idea.

Strategies to Use

Based on findings from the Wabash National Study and my own experiences, I developed the following strategies for using juxtaposition to facilitate integration of learning.

Class Discussions

In faculty work, traditional class discussions are a good way to open conversations among students to explore divergent ideas. Establishing ground rules for a respectful exchange before you get started will help the discussion go smoothly. Likewise, agreeing on a minimum or maximum number of times each student should participate in the discussion can ensure that no individual dominates the conversation and that all students have a voice. Remember the principles of cognitive dissonance: Students who are experiencing the most dissonance will try to avoid information that will increase that dissonance. Acknowledge this and try to keep all students involved in the discussion even if they are uncomfortable with the conflicting information. If students quickly come to a consensus on one idea, or a few vocal individuals dominate the discussion, you may want to play devil's advocate and introduce new ideas or dilemmas to the discussion.

Play Devil's Advocate

As an educator, you can intentionally put conflicting ideas side by side and encourage students to think about them, weigh the concepts using criteria they have established, and consider how the ideas might come together. Complicating the discussion is a tactic that can disrupt the process of group think that can often happen in courses or organizations and encourage new voices to enter the conversation.

In facilitating group discussions with graduate students in higher education administration, I will often intentionally disagree with them regardless of the position they take to force them to look at a different perspective and work with it. For example, I might ask students to role-play and assume the role of a university administrator. Then I prompt them to describe how they would respond to the parents' phone call about their college student's involvement in a campus protest. Then I will ask them to respond to a similar call from the university president, and then another similar phone call about the protest from a state policymaker. Requiring students to juxtapose these varied perspectives helps them integrate learning and practice communicating with multiple audiences as a college administrator.

Magolda and Baxter Magolda (2011) and Magolda, Baxter Magolda, and Carducci (2019) masterfully modeled juxtaposition as an educational strategy. In these two volumes, the editors paired chapters in a series of contested issues in higher education, for example, the relevance of identity centers on campus (offices for women, racial and ethnic groups, LGBTQ students, etc.), curbing alcohol abuse, and setting professional boundaries. The two chapters on each topic take different approaches to the issue, introducing different perspectives and discussing the nuances of the situation. A series of reflective questions following the two chapters examines the complexity and heightens the cognitive dissonance of the topic. Each topic also included a reading list and the URL that links to a blog to support those who want to learn more about the issue or interact with others who share an interest in the topic.

Practice Makes Perfect

Intentionally practice juxtaposition for integration with students. Put two different things or ideas together and challenge students to integrate them with targeted prompts. Start simple with two items, for example, a pencil and a school bus. How are these two connected? (They are both yellow, and they are both related to education.) How can you apply learning from one to the other? (I use the bus to get to school, where I write with my pencil; I use my pencil to draw a picture of the school bus.) How might you synthesize these two? (Admittedly, synthesis is challenging with simple nouns, but you might develop a story that includes the pencil and the bus, bringing them together in the narrative.) Continue this activity regularly with more and more complex ideas and statements.

Another more complex exercise that I use in my course on college student development theory is to put several related developmental theories together and ask students to discuss how they are similar, different, and have influenced one another. For example, examining the identity and psychosocial development theories of Erikson (1950), Marcia (1966), and Josselson (1987) and discussing how these theories evolved from one other. Marcia refined and built on Erikson's model of eight ego identity statuses, adding more flexibility to the model. Josselson later built on the work of Erikson and Marcia by incorporating the experiences of women into the theory. Using this example, I can facilitate robust discussions about how the theorists connected, applied, and synthesized knowledge in each iteration of identity theory. This exercise models the integration of the learning process so that students become familiar with it and can do it on their own.

Passive Programming

Educators can also use juxtaposition in passive programming such as bulletin boards in residence halls, classroom buildings, or digital spaces. Creating displays that intentionally put two disparate ideas side by side can prompt reflection, comparison, and integration. Including simple prompts on the display such as "Where do you see similarities?" or "How does your experience relate?" can nudge students to consider their own experiences and how they line up with new information. Residence life professionals are notoriously good with passive programming in residence halls and have a powerful platform in their communities to facilitate integration of learning with creative and intentional displays.

Debates

Debating is an exercise that educators can use to more formally structure a class or organization discussion. However, whereas open discussion can generate many diverse ideas, it also has the potential to move quickly into group think and allow the loudest perspectives to dominate, marginalizing some students or ideas. In a structured debate, you can assign positions to students and instruct them to argue for that perspective whether or not it aligns with their personal beliefs. This exercise serves multiple purposes: It requires students to consider and possibly argue in favor of ideas different from their own, it provides time in a class or organizational meeting for students to hear a variety of perspectives, and it structures speaking time, giving students who may not speak up in an organic conversation the time and platform to speak to their peers. Educators can also group students intentionally into diverse teams, further enriching the discussion and potential for integration of learning. Debates have a long history in U.S. higher education. They were used in early classrooms in colonial colleges (Kraus, 1961) and were also a common activity in the first cocurricular student organizations, which were often literary societies. The first fraternities also included debates as a part of their regular meetings, with two members presenting different sides of an argument to the members (Richards, 2017; Voorhees, 1945).

Study Abroad or Away

Study abroad entails going to another country, whereas study away is a domestic experience in a city, state, or region different from one's own

(Sobania & Braskamp, 2009). Physically going to a different place is a great way to juxtapose students' day-to-day life and the culture of their home campus with the sights, sounds, smells, and culture of a new region or nation. Studying abroad or away puts students in direct contact with different languages, norms, and daily schedules. Some students may find this experience exhilarating, but others may be challenged by the notion that their way of life is not the only, nor necessarily the best, way to do things.

Reading List and Syllabus

As a faculty member, you have control over the syllabus or reading list for your group. Think about the materials you include and consider juxtaposing different perspectives in the resources. Adding books, articles, videos, or podcasts that represent diverse ideas can set up the class for some of the discussions, debates, or assignments that use juxtaposition to promote integration. Likewise, consider the authors of the works you include as well as their content. Are your materials representative across gender, race, sexuality, and national origin? Pairing different ideas, identities, and historical eras on your syllabus can spark lively discussions that can lead students to connect, apply, and synthesize their learning across contexts.

Demonstration

Show students two different yet equally effective solutions to the same problem, and ask students to discuss the two approaches. This exercise overlaps juxtaposition with hands-on practice in that students can physically try two competing ways of doing something. It demonstrates to students that there is not one right answer to a question and establishes examples for students to relate to their own life experiences. This exercise may work well with student athletes to demonstrate a variety of techniques that can be employed to meet a goal. It can also be effective in teaching writing to demonstrate there is more than one way to write a convincing, well-researched paper, and there is no particular formula to rely on for good writing at the college level and beyond.

Summary

In this chapter, I explored the ways juxtaposition serves to promote integration of learning for college students. Introducing disparate perspectives for college students to consider and grapple with can prompt cognitive dissonance and ultimately integration. Classroom discussions are a common environment for juxtaposition, with students and instructors exchanging ideas on a topic and then debating the merits of these approaches. Comparing different ideas is a common student response to juxtaposition; compare and contrast is necessary but not sufficient for integration of learning. For students to truly integrate, they must go beyond a simple comparison of two ideas or perspectives to find a relationship that becomes a connection, application, or synthesis.

Reflection Questions: Things to Think About in Your Educational Practice

Take a few minutes to read and reflect on the following questions. Jot down your thoughts on paper, your phone, your laptop, or wherever is convenient. Be as formal or informal as you like in how you respond; the important thing is that you give yourself time to reflect.

1. Can you recall being faced with juxtaposed concepts as an undergraduate student? What did it feel like? What approach did you take to the juxtaposition?
2. Where are the prime locations for juxtaposition in your work with students? Identify two or three spaces where you can embrace juxtaposition.
3. What contrasts in your work can you share with students to illustrate juxtaposition in everyday life? How can you help students think about these contrasts with an integrative lens, approaching ideas thinking how they can bring these together in their mind?
4. How diverse are the readings and resources you provide to students? Is there space for juxtaposing ideas in the materials you work with over the course of a semester or year?
5. How can you bring the idea of juxtaposing into your work with students?

7

PRACTICE 4

Hands-On Experiences

Experiences that promote integration of learning for college students are often hands-on or immersive, including programs with a residential component such as living learning communities, a growing trend in university housing and residence life (Brower & Inkelas, 2010; Inkelas, Jessup-Anger, Benjamin, & Wawrzynski, 2018). Study abroad or study away experiences were discussed frequently by students in the Wabash National Study of Liberal Arts Education interviews. However, study abroad courses and living learning communities are by no means the only hands-on experiences that promote integration of learning; alternative breaks, in-class experiments, local field trips, service-learning, peer tutoring, and many other experiences can also offer the deep immersion characteristic of the hands-on practices. By taking students out of their familiar surroundings and comfort zones and immersing them in a new and different context, students are challenged to reconcile new observations and ways of seeing the world with what they have previously known.

My own experiences with study abroad have been transformational. I first studied abroad in Kraków, Poland, in 1994 as part of a summer program in economics. The Iron Curtain had recently fallen, and Poland was in the midst of the transition from a planned communist economy to a market system. It was not a particularly luxurious study abroad destination, but it was the most affordable option available to me. This was my first time traveling overseas, and I thought it might be my only chance to go abroad in my life, so I wanted to do and see as much as I possibly could.

I was 20 years old, and this was my first time experiencing a culture different from my own. I had studied the Polish language in a one-credit preparation course before the program but didn't have any mastery aside from being able to ask for the restroom, say please and thank you, and order a beer (*piwo, proszę*). I learned quickly that plenty of people in the world did not speak English and got along just fine, contrary to my U.S.-centric view of the world.

On arrival in Kraków, my U.S. classmates and I were immersed in Polish life. We lived in a student residence hall named Dom Merkury (Mercury House) and shared a suite with students from Italy and The Netherlands. We had all our meals in the university cafeteria or at local restaurants. It was necessary to learn the local bus system to navigate the city and get from point A to point B. These day-to-day situations demanded putting my limited language skills to use, and I learned more words and phrases in Polish to get what I wanted and needed. I was immersed in the environment and had to quickly apply what I had learned before the trip to my everyday life. I was constantly learning new things and had to integrate these new insights, words, and lenses to better function in my role as a student and in my life in Kraków.

Hands-on experiences involve students physically by demanding a certain level of performance; students have to do something. In addition, these experiences are often immersive, such as study away, residence life, or work and internships. Some hands-on experiences happen one time in one place, like an experiment in a chemistry class, for example. Others, however, surround students and become a part of their daily life 24 hours, 7 days a week, such as intercollegiate athletics, living learning communities, and service-learning alternative breaks. Hands-on experiences can change students' normal daily routines with new schedules, foods, sleep patterns, people, and rituals to create a new normal for daily life. These deeply engaging practices serve as a structure to introduce students to a specific routine and way of life that is different from what they are used to.

Hands-on experiences are challenging in part because students can't easily retreat; apart from quitting an internship, moving to a new residence hall, or flying home from study abroad, a student must persist in the experience even if it is difficult or challenges the student's perspectives. Learning from these experiences is often intense and can be difficult to integrate with previous learning because it is overwhelming. These immersive experiences lead to integration of learning that happens slowly over time and can be difficult, for example, during the challenging reentry time after returning from study abroad. The downside is that it is easy to compartmentalize such immersive experiences because they are often so different from the student's normal life or experience.

How Do Hands-On Experiences Help Students Integrate Learning?

Hands-on experiences allow students to put what they are learning into action by demanding they perform and requiring them to play an active role. At times, these experiences put pressure on students to try something new, perhaps interacting with someone different, trying a new skill or technique, or using a software application for the first time. In many cases, these hands-on experiences require students to move outside the comforts of their usual experiences. These new experiences and environments can be disorienting to students, and this is in part what makes them so powerful.

In our analysis of Wabash National Study data (Barber & King, 2014), we found the following developmental pathways that college students used as they responded to the demands of developmentally effective experiences: (a) act to resolve discomfort or (b) seek structures to cope. This is a developmental version of fight or flight: I am going to stick it out and see what I can do (seeking support, using a foreign language, trying to fit in), or I am going to get out of this situation (leaving the program or changing the environment in some way).

The idea of a disorienting dilemma is relevant here in a literal sense. Mezirow's (1991) book on transformative learning discussed the idea of disorientation as key to learning. This is particularly applicable in study away or study abroad experiences in which a student is physically located somewhere new and often unfamiliar and is expected to adapt. I don't assume that all hands-on experiences that promote integration are disorienting (or vice versa). An internship, for example, may be a new experience but not necessarily disorienting. Likewise, experiences such as service-learning, leadership positions, and changing academic majors can be quite disorienting.

The reality of a hands-on learning experience is the pressure in the moment to perform and the expectation of action. Students might take immediate action to try to alleviate this pressure, either through clear success or doing well enough to take some of the pressure away (fake it till you make it). Or they might pause and seek support to address the demanding situation. In other words, students don't take immediate action; for example, they might not know what to do in the moment, but they search for structures (organizations, family, counselors, peer support groups, etc.) to help them handle the pressure and move toward success.

Two characteristics—difficult retreat and daily life—are typical of hands-on experiences that promote integration of learning like study abroad, work or internships, and residential communities. Because they become so much a part of life, it is probable that students will bring together prior knowledge with the new knowledge gained through these experiences.

Difficult Retreat

Hands-on experiences are difficult to retreat from. Part of the challenge and excitement of a study abroad or study away experience is that you are living in a new culture for a period of time; it could be one week, or it could be one year, but for the designated time, you eat, sleep, and breathe in a place different from home. Living learning communities have a similar aspect in that it is where you live. Unless you deliberately avoid it, the community is a part of your daily life. This is true of all residential experiences to some extent—they are a part of your daily life.

Daily Life

Residence life is also a powerful daily life learning experience for students in the Wabash National Study. The residential experience provides key hands-on experiences such as resolving conflicts, working with diverse others, and the day's learning. Greenleaf College had residential learning communities that were another powerful example of hands-on, immersive learning. First-year Greenleaf students enrolled in linked courses with others in their residence hall. These courses shared not only the same students and location but also points of connection in terms of the content and assignments. This begs the question of how to provide students who live off campus with similar experiences. Research has shown that the majority of college students begin their undergraduate careers in off-campus housing (Kelchen, 2018). We know that the residential experience can be a crucible for integration of learning, so how can we as educators make use of that residential experience even when students live off campus?

The Role of Reflection in Hands-On Experiences

Hands-on experiences are exciting learning opportunities because they're action-packed. Students are living in diverse cultures, building new structures, and working in communities. Students are immersed in the experience, and they are learning by doing. It can be difficult to pause the action in hands-on experiences to take time to reflect and make meaning of what is being learned. Often, reflection is missed altogether because students (and faculty/staff) are tired after an intense hands-on experience. However, I argue that the quiet space of reflection is a necessary companion to the motion of hands-on experiences. For many of the students in the Wabash National Study, reflection came in part though the interviews in which they participated for the study. In this section, I share examples of how student activities, internships, and service-oriented alternative breaks can facilitate integration of learning.

In the first example, Elliot, a first-year student at Wabash College, talked about integration of learning outside the classroom and how he used his previous interests and skills acquired at home in building a homecoming float in college:

> I'm good with my hands. I'm not an excellent artist by any means, but I feel like I can draw decently. My dad's an operations manager at a construction company, but he worked his way up from working in the lumber yards so he's developed skills . . . like he's built countertops for our home. I've always helped him out in that. (Elliot, Wabash College, Year 1)

The interviewer, then asked, "So can you think back to the past, when did you realize that you had these skills or you had the first memory of realizing [that] hey, I'm pretty good at this?" and Elliot responded:

> I can't put my finger on a first memory, but I've always liked to do puzzles. . . . Not just you know pieces of puzzles in general, but mind puzzles. I don't know if you are familiar with the Sudokus, in the newspaper. I thoroughly enjoy doing those. I really like those a lot so it kind of transfers over into thinking of the many different things that can go on a piece of paper. Different ways the float could have been constructed. . . . I've done things like that in the past, so [I] can also go back to my past experiences knowing what I've done in similar situations and [apply] them to the now. (Elliot, Wabash College, Year 1)

Elliot revealed that application is not limited to the academic arena as he used his love of Sudoku and past experience in carpentry with his dad to assist with the construction of his fraternity's homecoming float.

It is increasingly common for college students to work or complete an internship during their undergraduate years. According to data from Georgetown University's Center on Education and the Workforce, nearly 14 million people, 70% to 80% of college students, are employed at least part-time (Carnevale et al., 2015). Many of those students are working much more; 40% of undergraduates worked at least 30 hours per week while in school. These employment experiences, internships, and full- or part-time work are excellent examples of hands-on education that can promote integration of learning.

Jade, a senior at St. Bernadette University, noted making connections between her internship work in marketing and her studies in sociology:

> Finding a target audience is very similar to what sociology does. And also
> ... I guess I've always been interested in how people [make] the assumptions they make about their audience and then the way ... companies try to feed into those assumptions, and [sometimes] they work and [sometimes] they don't work. So in the marketing and advertising field I got to be on the other end of that. (Jade, St. Bernadette University, Year 4)

This shows that she was able to apply her learning in sociology to help her understand the nature of marketing.

Short-term, service-oriented study away experiences have also been proven to promote integration of learning. Niehaus et al. (2017) found that among 38 participants in an alternative break program, all experienced some form of integration of learning related to the trip. Analyzing interview data from the National Survey of Alternative Breaks, they found that connection ($n = 348$) was the most frequent integrative approach used by students, followed by application ($n = 98$), and then synthesis ($n = 22$). Related to the notion of hands-on practices, they noted in their study that

> one particularly important form of connection was the links that many students were able to make between their ABs [alternative breaks] and their own communities; ABs are often not isolated experiences for students, but rather experiences that contribute to students' continued commitment to service. (p. 19)

The impact of being immersed in an alternative break curriculum produced integrative learning that persisted 1.5 to 2.5 years after the alternative break experience (Niehaus et al., 2017).

This is not to imply that one-time hands-on experiences don't promote integration of learning as well. An experiment in class, a day trip to a new community, and a service-learning project are also hands on and have a similar effect of drawing on what we know and linking it to the new experience. This is what Kolb (1984) called concrete experience, the act of doing something, which is the first step in his cycle of experiential education (followed by reflective observation, abstract conceptualization, and active experimentation). For example, a field trip to a synagogue for a Christian student may be a one-time experience that involves physically going to a new space, observing or interacting with people who are different, and taking in new sounds, scents, and views, using all of their senses. This concrete experience for the student is followed by a period of reflecting on what was experienced (reflective observation); making meaning of what was experienced, perhaps in relation to the student's own faith or spiritual practices (abstract conceptualization); and trying new experiences in other settings (active experimentation). In this example, active experimentation might be visiting services at a mosque or another Christian denomination that is different from one's own following the visit to the synagogue.

Hands-On Experiences in the Integration of Learning Model

In this section, I explore how the three approaches to integration of learning (connection, application, and synthesis) appear in hands-on experiences. (See Table 7.1 for a summary of hands-on experiences and Table 9.1 for a comprehensive planning matrix that compiles information from all five research-based practices to facilitate integration of learning.)

Connection

Connection in the practice of hands-on experiences involves students experimenting with putting ideas into action. In this category of integration,

TABLE 7.1
Hands-On Experience Practice: Student Experience by Integrative Approach

Practice	*Connection*	*Application*	*Synthesis*
Hands-on experiences	Students have an idea that knowledge can be used in the world and an initial awareness that lessons learned in principle can be enacted in real life. It is trial and error in terms of implementing knowledge and skills in the real world, some failures build a foundation for future successes. Students immersed in a new context or experience for the first time may scramble to find any similarities or comfort.	Students put learned knowledge and skills into action, realizing they have agency to do something that brings an idea into the real world. They have a sense of ability to act but are not yet entirely comfortable or confident.	Students can choose knowledge and skills appropriate to a changing situation. Students have a sense of independence in their own abilities and can modify and combine learning from multiple contexts to meet the demands of the situation at hand. Students bring together information and skills from different environments or cultures.

students have an idea that knowledge is important, but they may not know how to use knowledge in their lived experience. Students might have an initial awareness that in principle lessons learned can be enacted in real life but they do not yet know how use the knowledge in practice. It can be a big leap from learning in principle to learning for practice. Students may need several attempts at connection before they find success, but the key is for them to recognize the possibility that learning can have a practical use and that ideas and knowledge can be translated into action. For students, connection at first may be noticing differences or what is missing from their home environment. An acknowledgment of what is missing from previous daily life is an initial step in replacing it with something else. It is a form of connecting two experiences to find out what is missing and figuring out what can replace it.

Application

Application in hands-on experience practice is when students put learned knowledge and skills into action and do something that brings an idea into the real world such as using a language learned in a course with an international visitor or on a trip to a new place. Another example is when students join a professional or cultural group outside campus for a class assignment and report to the class on their experiences. Amber, a sophomore at Azalea College, said her communications courses provided a new framework and new language to examine societal messages more critically:

> I'm more critical, because . . . my different classes make me look at things differently. . . . My gender and communication class makes me look at everything from a . . . critical perspective and [ask] how is this sexist? Is this sexist? How [is] this affecting this, so that I can pass a billboard and [say] that is so sexist. Why do they do that, look like that? . . . I just look at things with a critical lens and a different perspective [for] different things. Sometimes, I'll be able to say something's not right . . . but I couldn't pinpoint why and now I'm like, okay, . . . this is how they're being sexist. (Amber, Azalea College, Year 2)

In this example, Amber applied the critical lens she learned about in class to view the world around her. Specifically, the hands-on approach promoted in her gender and communication course prompted her to use a critical perspective in other contexts. As a result, she began to look at everything using this lens.

Synthesis

Synthesis in hands-on experiences practice occurs when students bring previous learning into a new context, use it to accomplish a goal and then modify their previous learning to accommodate the new experience and perhaps different conditions. In synthesis, the student is adept at drawing on information learned in multiple contexts and applying it in new ways. This new way of doing things continues to be adjusted as new experiences happen in real life. For example, in the context of a study abroad experience, this manifests itself in a student becoming independent in the new environment and creating a daily life in a new place.

Dolores, a junior at Golden State University, explained how she built on what she learned in her business management major to start her own financial service business. She noted that when clients come to her office, she trains them on the products and services that are available and the current conditions of the market:

> And so I'm able to use that [work experience] as a huge boost for myself, as well as the school education that I get in classes . . . in my accounting class we're learning right now about job order processing and more business leadership, business ownership. And so I'm able to put those both [work experience and school education] together and get above the rest because some people only use one or the other. (Dolores, Golden State University, Year 3)

Dolores described how her coursework in business management and the hands-on experience of starting her own business as a college student came together in a way that enhanced her business and her formal education. One without the other would not have been as rich or fulfilling an experience for her.

For another illustration of the three approaches to integration in a hands-on experience, let's use the example of my experience as an undergraduate studying abroad in Poland. Connection was realizing that what I learned in class had a tangible reality, that what I read about or saw in media really existed. An extreme example of this was my traveling 24 hours each way on a bus across Europe to see the Eiffel Tower in person and make the connection that it existed in reality and not just on TV. Application was using the Polish language skills I learned in class to order dinner in Kraków. Finally, synthesis was getting to a point where I was comfortable and confident walking to class or to the dorm by myself in Poland and understanding the patterns of daily life in my new environment. This new way of seeing the world ignited in me a desire to travel that has never gone away after that trip to Poland as an undergraduate.

With study abroad, reentry to the students' home campus is a key point for synthesis; this is when they merge what they learned in an international context with their domestic environment. Combining learning from often disparate contexts is challenging, and sometimes students end up compartmentalizing learning from their experiences abroad. Useem and Downie (1976) provided another example of synthesis as the children in their book are expatriates living in a foreign country and bring together their home culture (where their family originated) with their host culture (where they are currently living, often for an extended time) into a third, synthesized culture.

Strategies to Use

How can you help students integrate learning through hands-on experiences? Based on the findings from the Wabash National Study and the research related to hands-on experiences in higher education, I have developed the following strategies for faculty members, administrators, and student affairs educators.

Provide Regular Opportunities to Put Ideas Into Action

Avoid lecturing at students and find ways for them to experience and use the ideas you're teaching them. Avoid the one-way street consisting of you, the educator, providing information and the students receiving it. I want to stress the qualifier *regular* for opportunities. Every class session, meeting, and assignment should include regular opportunities for hands-on application. Don't fill face-to-face meetings with didactic lectures that students could read or watch as a video. Whether it is a class session, organization meeting, or otherwise, make your meeting worth the time of convening.

Ask Frequently How This Relates to Life Outside College

Sometimes it is easy to get lost in explanations of theory or big ideas and lose the relevance of learning to day-to-day experience. Use hands-on experiences to reinforce the main concepts, and ask students explicitly how they can use the ideas you are teaching in their life outside college, for example,

- How are you connecting these ideas to others you already know? (Connect)
- How are you using these ideas and skills in real life? (Apply)
- How do these ideas and skills come together with what you already know? (Synthesize)

Change Space and Place

Often, our regular interactions with students happen in the same physical places: a classroom, our office, a conference room, a residence hall lounge. Shake things up and move the meeting or class to a new location and incorporate that location into their learning. Moving to a different physical location emphasizes to students the notion that learning happens everywhere and can help prompt integration of learning by demonstrating that links can be made in learning across contexts. It shows that learning is not bounded by the walls of a classroom or even the boundaries of a university campus. Living learning communities excel with this strategy because they bring faculty, staff, and students together for academic experiences outside the traditional classroom. They invite students to continue class discussions in residential spaces and may provide work or living space for faculty or staff to encourage the development of long-term relationships between students and educators.

Consider Maker Spaces

Popularized in part by the design thinking movement, maker spaces are increasingly common on college and university campuses. The use of physical materials to brainstorm and build prototype models of ideas allows student to bring together the abstract and the concrete. Students literally use their hands to make integration. These models are conceived as a solution to a problem like designing the ideal wallet or creating the backpack of the future. By using a real-world issue while providing students with physical materials and supplies to try to solve the problem or improve on the existing product, maker spaces are an opportunity for students to integrate learning in a way they can immediately see.

Engage Multiple Senses

Traditional lecture-style instruction engages two senses: hearing and seeing. Hands-on experiences can enlist all five senses in the learning process. Students might taste new foods in a study abroad program, touch an animal in a biology lesson, or smell the odor of a chemical reaction in a chemistry experiment. These examples go beyond watching and listening to an educator explain an experience or idea. As engaging as a faculty member might be, having a hands-on experience is markedly different from listening to someone talk about it. Additional senses can help students relate their new learning to previous experience by similar scents, textures, or flavors.

Create Disorienting Dilemmas for Students

In developing course curricula, incorporate hands-on experiences that will challenge students and push them outside their comfort zone. Propose difficult questions that don't have a right answer. King and Kitchener (1994) called these ill-structured problems and demonstrated how they helped students advance to more complex forms of moral reasoning. Likewise, Mezirow (1991) credited such disorienting dilemmas for transformative learning for college students.

Use Role-Playing

Role-playing, a hands-on experience in which students take on the identity of someone else, also overlaps with the embracing diversity and identity practice for integration of learning discussed in chapter 8. The development of empathy—meeting, living with, talking to, and collaborating with others who are different from us—allows us to integrate new concepts into our existing ways of thinking and helps us imagine what it must be like to be someone else, and we begin to see multiple perspectives. In role-playing, we can take that emerging empathy and try it on like a new skin. What would this other person feel in this situation?

A popular activity in residence life student staff training is Behind Closed Doors. In this activity students take on the roles of resident assistants and students who are misbehaving or in crisis to simulate the challenging situations resident assistants face in their day-to-day work with those in their buildings. Common scenarios include policy enforcement such as addressing a noise complaint, reporting underage drinking, and submitting work orders for repairs. However, more serious situations such as responding to self-harm, sexual assault, and eating disorders are often included to role-play how to counsel and refer peers who need additional support.

Summary

In this chapter, I discussed the ways hands-on, immersive educational experiences can promote integration of learning for college students. Traditional experiences such as study abroad and residential living have characteristics of hands-on experiences as well as more recent additions to the higher education landscape, such as short-term alternative breaks and maker spaces. In the next chapter, I examine how college educators can cultivate diverse learning environments and encourage students to bring their identities into learning experiences.

Reflection Questions: Things to Think About in Your Educational Practice

Take a few minutes to read and reflect on the following questions. Jot down your thoughts on paper, your phone, your laptop, or wherever is convenient. Be as formal or informal as you like in how you respond; the important thing is that you give yourself time to reflect.

1. When did you have an experience as an undergraduate that was hands-on? Jot down some notes about what you recall about that experience. What did you learn from it?
2. How can you provide hands-on experiences for the students you work with?
3. In your role as an educator, how can you create immersive experiences that challenge students' assumptions and current perspectives?
4. How can you collaborate with other professionals outside your area to create hands-on experiences for students to learn; for example, student affairs collaborating with academic affairs, the business community, non-profits, or the government sector to break down the silos.
5. How can you incorporate at least one disorienting dilemma into your work with students? What support will you offer to help students navigate this challenge?
6. What learning experiences or places can you build into daily life for your students? For yourself?

8

PRACTICE 5

Embrace Diversity and Identity

Simply stated, we learn better in diverse groups; to integrate learning, you must have disparate ideas and perspectives to integrate. Undergraduate students come to college with rich histories and complex identities. However, often their identities are not invited into their experiences inside and outside the classroom, overlooking prior knowledge that may be critical to the learning at hand.

Colleges and universities are increasingly diverse environments for student learning (Gurin et al., 2004), yet residential communities in the United States remain relatively homogeneous. Students often find themselves in racially diverse classrooms and residential environments for the first time when they come to college (Barber, 2010).

Who we are affects how we learn and vice versa. The main concept in this chapter has two components: First, it is important to create, foster, and support diverse learning environments, and second, it is important to acknowledge students' identities and encourage them to bring their whole selves into learning experiences.

Beatriz, second-generation Mexican American and a senior at St. Bernadette University who studied abroad in Mexico her junior year, described the connections she made with her identity and language skills in her Wabash National Study of Liberal Arts Education interview. Beatriz taught English in Mexico and subsequently started teaching English as a second language courses at her university when she returned to the United States:

> I really identified with so many things when I was in Mexico. And I saw a lot of aspects of myself that I didn't realize were rooted in Mexican culture, I just thought they were . . . my own little quirk or something that I have taken from my family. . . . And so I felt that I found a lot of myself in

Mexico and especially being here at [St. Bernadette] and [with] a population that's essentially homogenous, meaning the White culture.... I think that [being in Mexico] was great in terms of [my] self-confidence and identity. It made me so much more passionate about my studies in Spanish and getting to know my culture more, and so that was definitely a huge aspect of [my time in Mexico]; just the personal growth that I experienced there.... The whole experience in Mexico was huge and that really helped me make so much more of a cultural connection, and it definitely [helped me] put a lot more emphasis on my family and my culture as a key value and as a key part of my identity. (Beatriz, St. Bernadette University, Year 4)

There is a lot to unpack in this quote from Beatriz, and it's emblematic of the complexity of issues of diversity and identity and the difficulty in separating one from the other. She remarked on the diversity (or lack thereof) at St. Bernadette, which perhaps was more apparent to her after her return from study abroad in Mexico. At the same time, Beatriz recognized her own identity as a Mexican American and realized the great impact her family's Mexican heritage had on her life.

Cultivating Diverse Learning Environments

In thinking about diverse learning environments, I define *diversity* broadly, not limited to racial or ethnic diversity. Diversity in gender, class, sexual orientation, faith, worldview, language, socioeconomic status, and other forms of difference also need to be considered. There may be great diversity to be uncovered at a single-sex college, historically Black college or university, or faith-based institution. It is not just a priority for the admission process; recruitment is certainly an area of significant impact. Educators also have tools at our disposal to attract different types of students to enroll in our courses, join organizations, and attend events and activities. For faculty members, do you allow non-major students to enroll in your courses? If so, how do you advertise your courses to students who may not be in your discipline? Where are you advertising your upcoming courses, and how do you help the organization that you advise to reach out to new members? For student affairs professionals, how do you work to create inclusive and equitable organizations and communities on your campus? Are there new approaches to recruiting students from different demographics to participate in activities?

In addition to recruitment, we have the ability to help students see the diversity in an existing group. You can work to create a culture in class where students feel comfortable sharing their identities and revealing the underlying diversity of the group. Finding ways to prompt conversations about students' backgrounds and lives outside the course or organization can be productive in uncovering aspects of the diversity among the students.

However, simply bringing together students from diverse backgrounds in a common course or organization is not enough. Structural diversity, meaning that different types of people are present, is necessary but not sufficient to promote integration of learning. If two disparate ideas are brought into the same room but do not interact, then those two ideas remain separate and isolated, and there is no connection, application, or synthesis. For diversity and identity to prompt integration of learning, interaction, conversation, and direct sharing of ideas, experiences, and perspectives must also be involved. As educators, we cannot just bring in students from different backgrounds and expect them to engage with one another. We must intentionally create environments where students feel safe to share their differences (King, Perez, & Shim, 2013). We must be intentional and skillful at promoting discussion and collaboration across difference to promote integration of learning.

Embracing Students' Identities

This leads me to the next big concept in this chapter: We need to acknowledge students' identities and encourage them to bring their whole selves into learning experiences. Educators must open the door for students to bring their identities into a course or experience. In previous educational settings, students may have been expected to leave their identities behind when they came into the school, so as college educators we need to make it clear that we encourage students to bring themselves fully into the classroom or campus.

When people can connect the learning objectives to who they are, they are more likely to learn (Baxter Magolda, 2003). Creating a link between the content of the course and the students' backgrounds can vastly improve the learning experience. This does not have to be a guessing game for the educator. It can be as simple as asking individual students how a particular concept or idea connects to their life growing up or giving students a few minutes in class to jot down ideas about how the course content links to their identity. It should not have to be a secretive process that tricks students into learning. It can (and should) be explicit, inviting students to bring their whole selves into the activity or assignment. This is creating an opportunity for holistic education.

However, the focus on diversity and identity is not intended only for students of minority status or who are marginalized in some way. There must be opportunity for students with majority identities to reflect on their majority identity and privilege. The students who are in the majority and are perhaps most in need of reflecting on their own identities are not doing so, and it limits their ability to integrate learning (Perez & Barber, 2017). Students with privileged identities (White, male, Christian, straight, etc.) need to be included in explorations of identity, power, and privilege, and not treated as the normal or default identity.

How Does Embracing Diversity and Identity Help Students Integrate Learning?

Diversity and identity are essential to integration of learning. Students in the Wabash National Study are part of an intentionally diverse group of participants. We chose to interview students at racially diverse campuses, single-sex institutions, and large and small public and private schools. In addition to selecting a range of campus environments to visit, we oversampled for students of color to ensure that a variety of perspectives were included in the study. Considering diversity and identity in relation to learning is important because we want students to be welcome fully as themselves. You can learn and integrate learning better when you are able to be your full self, draw on previous experience, and link to other contexts including home, work, and previous educational institutions.

Multiple Dimensions of Identity

The model of multiple dimensions of identity (Abes, Jones, & McEwen, 2007) is helpful in considering why identity is so important to integration of learning. The reconceptualized model positions a person's core identity, those most closely held values, beliefs, and characteristics, at the center of an atomlike structure with the person's various social identities circling that core like electrons. Gender, race, sexual orientation, language, faith, worldview, citizenship, and so on are in motion, and depending on one's environment, certain identities are more salient and come to the surface. For example, students taking a gender studies course may find their gender to be a salient identity in the context of that class meeting such as discussing gender, investigating issues from a gendered perspective, and so on. In another context later that same day, gender might not be as salient for a student, and perhaps another dimension of identity rises to the surface and is prominent. In this model, although there is a stable core personality, the way identity is communicated and performed is fluid and influenced by context and environment.

Figure 8.1. Reconceptualized model of multiple dimensions of identity.

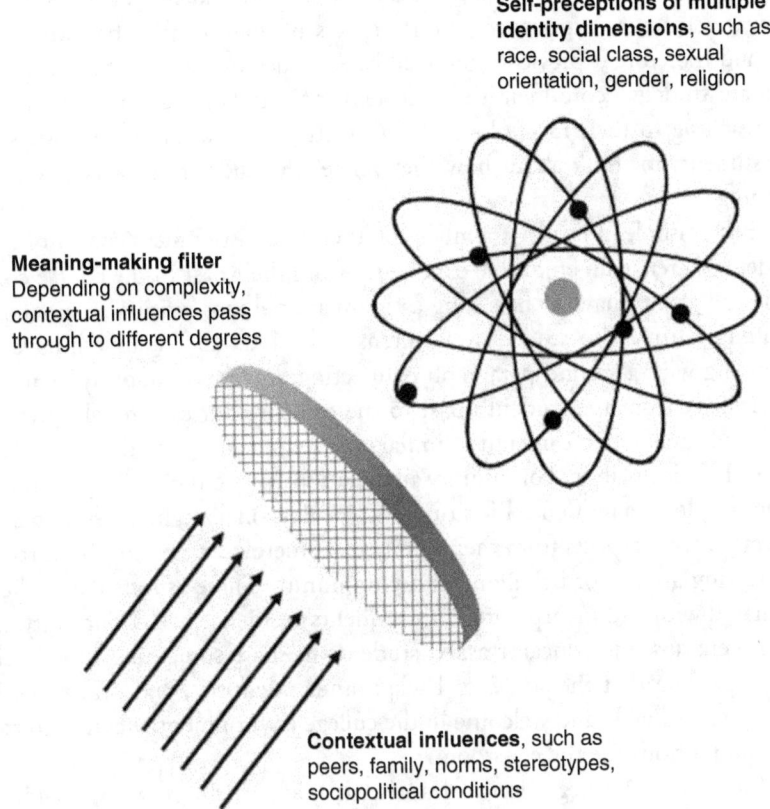

Note. From "Reconceptualizing the Model of Multiple Dimensions of Identity: The Role of Meaning-Making Capacity in the Construction of Multiple Identities," by E. S. Abes, S. R. Jones, & M. K. McEwen, 2007, *Journal of College Student Development, 48*(1), p. 7. Copyright 2007 by SAGE. Reprinted with permission.

Identity is also mediated by the meaning-making level in the multiple dimensions of identity model (see Figure 8.1; Abes et al., 2007). Represented as a screen, people's meaning-making determines the extent external influences affect how they see themselves. If someone has a less complex way of making meaning, the screen is more porous, and external voices have a stronger impact on identity. In other words, what other people think of us matters a lot. However, if a person has a more complex meaning-making structure, the screen is tighter and less porous, effectively blocking out some of the external voices and allowing the person to listen to their internal voice and express identity without as much concern for the opinions of others or society writ large and to express an identity that is more representative of the person's core.

So what does this tell us about integration of learning? The educational experiences and environments we create can influence identity, and based on how we structure experiences, some aspects of identity may be more salient and therefore expressed more readily. As educators, we must respect and validate students' core identities and help them to connect the content we are teaching to their most closely held identities. Look for creative ways to get students to think about how they relate who they are to what they are learning.

For example, a faculty member could craft an assignment that prompts students to relate an enjoyable experience from their past to the course content. It does not have to be a long assignment, perhaps writing a paragraph recalling a time the student was intensely curious about something and following with a second paragraph connecting, however tenuously, that joy of curiosity from the student's past to the current course material. Student affairs administrators can craft a similar activity to prompt students to relate deeply held ideas about community and relationships to their college context. For example, in a residence life situation, a professional might ask students to reflect on what aspects from their family or hometown were most important to creating a sense of belonging and community. These aspects could then be shared with and incorporated into students' residence hall community. In both scenarios, the educator asked students to share something from their past, signaling that the students' backgrounds, identities, and prior experiences were valuable and welcome in the college environment, whether in the classroom or outside the classroom.

Like identity, integration of learning is mediated by meaning-making. Students with a less complex way of making meaning, that is, more externally defined, tend to focus on connection and application and may integrate less frequently. The voices of external authorities have a stronger influence on what and how students integrate.

In addition, these students are more reliant on the opinions of others for validation of identity. Sending strong external messages from an authority (e.g., a college educator) that students have valuable knowledge, relevant prior experience, and can integrate learning across contexts is internalized by those students. If you tell students they can integrate learning, they are likely to believe you, try it, practice it, and develop their ability.

Intergroup Relations

Intergroup relations (IGR) is a field of research and action that has a long history of bringing together diverse and often conflicting groups of people to engage in civil dialogue. As discussed earlier, it is not enough to simply assemble a diverse group of students; ideally, we want students to interact, build relationships, and learn from one another's experience. The growing body of literature on IGR is helpful in thinking about how to structure experiences to foster productive interactions.

Beginning in the early 1980s, IGR was used to facilitate relationships among groups that do not see eye to eye on issues, for example Jews and Arabs, heterosexual and LGBTQ people, and people with different racial identities. This body of work relates directly to integration of learning because at its core, IGR is about finding connections between seemingly incompatible beliefs. This concept of finding common ground is also central to integration of learning. As such, the skills and techniques of IGR can be useful for discussion in classes or in student organizations to help students learn how to listen to opposing views, engage in civil conversation with others who may disagree, and seek common understanding. These skills learned through IGR are also helpful in facilitating integration of learning.

The roots of IGR and education lie in the progressive philosophies of educators such as John Dewey, Paolo Freire, and Myles Horton. Their experiential pedagogies were holistic, seeking to break away from the traditional classroom lecture. According to Maxwell and Thompson (2017), "They emphasized learner-centered pedagogies that underscored the connections between personal experiences and conceptions of the social environment as significant steps to meaning-making" (p. 2).

IGR is one way to promote perspective taking, an important aspect of development. Perspective taking is a crucial link between identity and diversity. It compels individuals to understand who they are and how they see themselves, and then put that identity aside to try to understand who someone else is. In this way, students may be able to glimpse the identity of someone different from them. They might also be able to see their own identity through someone else's eyes.

The Role of Reflection in Embracing Diversity and Identity

I want to return to the idea of reflection discussed in chapter 3. Reflection can be helpful in embracing identity and diversity in several ways. Students do not always know how to make the time or space to reflect on their own identities and the ways they interact with diverse others. Those students who are in the majority and enjoy the most privilege often are the least aware of identity (Perez & Barber, 2017). Likewise, reflection can help individuals to be aware of the composition of groups in which they spend time. This may be on the large scale, such as the student body of a university, or a smaller scale, such as the membership of a fraternity or sorority. Making time in class or as a part of student activities for reflection is key. Often, students will not reflect on their own. In addition to providing the time and space for reflection, educators can offer prompts that specifically get at issues of identity and diversity to spark students' own thinking about these concepts.

Perspective taking is a developmental marker. Not all college students, and not all adults, can do this yet. We can't assume in the college context that students can do this well or at all when we first encounter them. Standing in someone else's shoes can be a powerful exercise for encouraging students to see multiple perspectives. However, before you can try on another's shoes, you must step out of your own. Trying to see the world from someone else's vantage point can be a challenging and sometimes frightening task. I suggest providing several spaces, public (e.g., class activities, discussions, organization meetings, service learning) and private (e.g., reflective journals, writing assignments), for students to experiment with perspective taking. Working to see an issue from an alternative point of view can help students clarify their own values and beliefs while gaining a greater understanding of others' values, beliefs, and life experiences (Barber, 2012).

Making time to reflect on your own identity and the power and privilege that may or may not accompany that identity is essential. Stepping outside one's own identity and looking at the world from another person's point of view is challenging and can be uncomfortable. However, it is necessary to be able to integrate learning. Students must be able to see multiple perspectives to relate them to one another and perhaps ultimately integrate them. Integration of learning is not ensured with multiple perspectives, but it helps. In Perez and Barber (2017), we found a significant overlap in experiences from students in the Wabash National Study that led to integration of learning and intercultural maturity. Creating learning environments with a diverse group of students and intentional attention to identity (one's own and that of others), provides an opportunity for students to practice perspective taking and wrestle with reconciling their experience with that of others.

Faith is an important aspect of personal identity (Small, 2011), and increasingly relevant in modern life in a diverse democracy. Faith is a defining characteristic of many institutions in the United States; about 1,000 colleges and universities are faith-based (Brown, 2016; National Center for Educational Statistics, 2018). At the same time, nearly one-third (currently 31.1%) of incoming first-year students identify themselves as agnostic, atheist, or otherwise secular (Stolzenberg et al., 2019). As educators, we have to navigate our own worldview identities, those of our students, and potentially the faith background of the institution where we work. Sometimes these align, but more often they do not.

For example, Owen, a senior at St. Bernadette University, chose a comparative religion major because of his experience of being an outsider as the only Catholic at a Protestant high school. He recalled,

> I remember being really kind of confused and kind of hurt and talking to my parents about it and ... anyway, it's sort of all stuff that I pushed aside for a long time. And at the time didn't realize why I was being left out sometimes. (Owen, St. Bernadette University, Year 4)

IGR activities build on an established foundation or research to bring students together in a way that encourages personal reflection and respectful exchanges of ideas. Beyond exposure to diverse perspectives, IGR and similar models show ways for students to engage with others who are different from them. In a nation and world that is increasingly diverse, these skills are paramount to community building and integrating learning.

Diversity and Identity in the Integration of Learning Model

Let us examine how the practice of embracing diversity and identity looks for the integration of learning approaches of connection, application, and synthesis.

Connection

Connection in the embracing diversity and identity practice involves having initial exposure to those who are different from oneself. This will look very different based on the context. If a campus is structurally diverse, students may meet diverse others frequently in classes, residence halls, and organizations. If the campus is more homogenous, diversity may be ideological or geographic rather than racial or ethnic. For connection, students gain an awareness that there are multiple perspectives; students should see that their own perspective is valid and valuable but know there are other perspectives that are also valid and valuable. Faculty and student affairs educators alike can ensure that students are comfortable bringing their home life and identity into classroom discussions, organizations, meetings, and so on and see that others can do so as well. It is important to go beyond simply occupying the same place to find something in common with another person, even if that person appears quite different. This connection may be a fleeting recognition of similarity, but it is a foothold for integration of learning.

Application

Application in the embracing identity and diversity practice involves students using lenses from an identity that is not their own to examine a problem or issue, for example, a male student using a feminist lens to examine public policy, or a White student employing critical theory to understand judicial reform. Students work together with those different from them on specific tasks or projects, which allows students to apply what they have learned about diverse others to building successful social and working relationships.

Application is also about using what you have learned about others' backgrounds, interests, and experiences to understand (or empathize with) multiple perspectives. This category is more concrete than connection; it involves putting what you have learned about diversity and identity into action.

Synthesis

In embracing the diversity and identity practice, synthesis involves students bringing together their own identity with what they've learned from diverse others; perhaps an aspect of personal identity is changed or developed as a consequence of interaction with diverse others. This may be acted on by creating a new identity in a diverse relationship or context.

Diana, a sophomore at Golden State University, shared her experience taking an Asian American History course as a first-year student. It was a large lecture course (100-plus students) that examined U.S. history from the perspective of Asian Pacific Islanders. Diana was the only African American student in the class. She appreciated her professor's teaching style; despite the large class size, he maintained eye contact with students, and he encouraged small-group discussion. Diana described the small group work as intimate:

> If you're sitting next to five people . . . in a group and [are] discuss[ing] this topic . . . work with people around you . . . [which makes] it seem more intimate than if it was [a] big classroom sitting there with other people just taking notes, so I think that was my favorite class last year. (Diana, Golden State University, Year 2)

In this course Diana formed close relationships with her classmates, most of whom were Asian American. She also applied her learning about Asian American history and perspectives to understand her own cultural history in a new way and for her to

TABLE 8.1
Diversity and Identity Practice: Student Experiences by Integrative Approach

Practice	Connection	Application	Synthesis
Diversity and identity	Students have initial exposure to others who have different identities and backgrounds; students are comfortable bringing their unique identity and previous experience into the educational environment. Students possess a general awareness that multiple perspectives exist.	Students can use lenses from an identity that is not their own to look at information, a problem, or an issue. Students can use knowledge of multiple perspectives to build social and working relationships with others who are different from themselves.	Students can bring together their own identity with the perspectives they have learned from diverse others; aspects of personal identity are changed as a consequence of interaction with diverse others.

get a kinship, a connection, and that's why I learned a lot of things I didn't know before. I didn't know about Filipinos and how they were looked at [negatively] when they came over to the States. . . . I just felt . . . even though we were from different ancestors [her Asian American classmates and herself as an African American], we were all the same because we went through the same. Our ancestors went through the same struggle. (Diana, Golden State University, Year 2)

In the synthesis process, students have a new, transformed view of their own identity as well as the identities of others. Bringing together aspects of understanding the complexities of identity and the experience of interacting with others who are different from themselves fosters a new appreciation for the benefits of diversity and how it enhances one's own identity. This appreciation for diversity becomes a part of one's identity, even when no individuals are no longer in diverse groups. Students seek diverse groups and readily recognize when groups are homogenous.

Table 8.1 is categorized by an integrative approach (connection, application, and synthesis) and summarizes the student perspective of embracing identity and diversity practice. Similar tables from the previous chapters are combined in Table 9.1 in a comprehensive integration of learning planning matrix, along with a discussion about creating an integrative curriculum.

Strategies to Use

How can you help students integrate by embracing diversity and identity? Based on the findings from the Wabash National Study and the research related to diversity and identity in higher education, I offer several practical strategies for faculty, administrators, and student affairs educators to use in their work.

Be Intentional About Groups and Pairing

Although it is time efficient to pair students with others sitting nearest to them for group work and sharing, this arrangement generally guarantees that students end up in conversations with people they already know and who are perhaps very similar to them. Dividing students into groups by having them count off is a way to randomize the composition of the groups and mix up those friends who may be sitting next to one another.

You could go a step further and intentionally create small groups, which is more time consuming for the instructor but ensures diverse groups based on the criteria you choose. These strategies will maximize the different experiences in group work and give students more ideas to integrate.

Set Ground Rules

To embrace diversity and identity and ultimately integrate learning, it is necessary for students to feel comfortable discussing aspects of their identities and asking appropriate questions to learn about others who are different from themselves (King et al., 2013). To facilitate this kind of interaction, college educators can establish ground rules and expectations for discussing sensitive topics about identity, including race, ethnicity, sexuality, faith, and worldview. It is helpful to acknowledge the fear students may feel; these topics are personal and unusual to discuss in a classroom or educational setting. However, great learning can come from having honest conversations about diversity and identity.

When I set expectations for these discussions in a class setting, I encourage students to ask questions even if they are not sure of the correct words. Hate speech, slurs, and derogatory language are off the table, but I do not want students to hold back from asking a question because they are not sure about using gay versus homosexual, or Caucasian versus White. We can learn about the appropriate and preferred terminology and language together, but that learning does not happen if students never join the discussion for fear of saying the wrong thing.

Share Aspects of Your Own Identity

Educators can encourage students to bring their full identities into the classroom by modeling the behavior. Sharing aspects of your own identity and background can help students understand you better as well as set an example for how others can integrate learning with their identities. I often tell students that I am a first-generation college (and graduate) student and talk about my experiences growing up to illustrate developmental theory in my own life. It is each educator's decision to disclose personal information, and there is less risk if you have a majority or privileged identity.

Ask Students About their Home and Experiences Growing Up

Show you are interested in students' identities by asking them about their experiences privately and publicly. Finding out about undergraduates' hometowns, high school experiences, and families gives you a fuller picture about that student's prior learning and signals to students that you have an interest in their experience outside the course or college context. Start with a confidential survey just for you as an educator to learn more about the backgrounds of the students in your class or group. Where did they grow up? What high school did they attend? How do they describe themselves in terms of race, gender, sexual orientation, national origin, and so on? What experiences in their past may be relevant to your course, organization, or activity? I ask students to complete a brief survey at the beginning of a semester to collect a few pieces of information about previous education and cocurricular experiences that I can follow up on with each student individually.

You do not want to single out a student in a large group by asking the student to share an aspect of their identity that the student may not want to discuss publicly, but it does allow the instructor to prime the pump and open a discussion by asking students to share their experiences. You might start out by saying, "I've talked with some of you about your high school experiences, and I want to encourage you to share some of those experiences in today's discussion." In most cases, once the first student reveals information about high school or family, others are eager to follow.

Welcome Students' Prior Learning

College students are not blank slates when they come to our campuses. They have at least 17 years of prior learning experiences and in some cases much more. Students need to know that you acknowledge, welcome, and validate this wealth of experience that makes up the student's identity. Baxter Magolda wrote about validating students' learning as a key tenet of the learning partnerships model (Baxter Magolda & King, 2004). It is essential in integration of learning for us to acknowledge the existing experience, knowledge, and skills to integrate them into the new learning that happens in your course or activity. Be explicit about your acknowledgment that students' prior experience has value and your expectation for them to integrate new learning with what they already know. This opens the door for students to bring their identities into the learning environment and encourages them to build on the foundation of learning they have established.

Recruiting for Diversity

You do not have to serve as an admissions officer to recruit for diversity. No matter your role on campus, you can actively work to bring diverse students together for educational experiences. Research shows that we learn better in diverse groups (Gurin et al., 2004; Hong & Page, 2004), therefore we need to prioritize diversity in our work. This may take the form of advertising your courses to a demographic of students who have not been represented in your class in the past, it might involve flyers, emails, or social media to get the word out; visiting a student organization to invite students to register; or updating your readings to be sure authors from a diversity of backgrounds are represented in the syllabus. For administrators, this may look like actively recruiting (and teaching undergraduates to recruit) from new student populations that are not heavily represented in their current membership or attendance. When we are intentional about convening diverse groups of students, we aid in integration of learning because students are exposed to new ideas that complement and perhaps challenge their existing knowledge. They are exposed to new ways of thinking that fuel integration.

Summary

Diversity and identity go hand in hand. As college educators, it is vital to strive to create diverse learning environments and embrace students' identities holistically. In the U.S. higher education context, students enter our institutions with varied exposure to diversity. Some come to campus from very homogenous residential and educational settings, and others are rooted in extremely diverse communities. As educators, faculty and student affairs administrators must work to link the content and habits of mind we are teaching to our students' identities; if students can relate personally to the material, they are likely to integrate that learning with their prior knowledge. This concludes the fifth and final practice for facilitating integration of learning. In the next chapter I explore how to bring these practices together using the integration of learning model to create an integrative curriculum for higher education.

Reflection Questions: Things to Think About in Your Educational Practice

Take a few minutes to read and reflect on the following questions. Jot down your thoughts on paper, your phone, your laptop, or wherever is convenient. Be as formal or informal as you like in how you respond; the important thing is that you give yourself time to reflect.

1. How comfortable were you as an undergraduate student bringing aspects of your identity, culture, and home life into your experiences in the classroom? Outside the classroom?
2. How welcoming do you consider your campus to be to students, faculty, and staff with diverse backgrounds?
3. How do you open the door for students to feel comfortable and confident bringing their whole selves into their educational experience?
4. As an educator, do you share aspects of your own identity with students? Why or why not? How can you do so?
5. How do you recruit students for your class, activities, or organization? What are your approaches to recruiting a diverse group of students for these educational experiences?

PART THREE

HOW TO MAKE IT STICK

9

CREATING AN INTEGRATIVE CURRICULUM

In Part Two (chapters 4–8), I discussed five research-based practices to facilitate integration of learning for college students. Part Three focuses on weaving these strategies into educators' practice to create an integrative curriculum and pedagogy. It is essential to have a mix of different ways of integrating (connection, application, and synthesis) as well as a variety of strategies. It is important to recall that in the integration of learning model as students become more complex learners they become adept at using all three ways of integrating in concert rather than abandoning less complex forms of integration for more advanced forms. By including several approaches to integration, college educators: (a) provide less advanced students with a place to get a foothold (connection, application) while offering a challenge to push them to develop (synthesis) and (b) provide more advanced students with an opportunity to use several ways of integrating learning.

Lattuca and Stark (2009) wrote about creating curricula for learning in traditional higher education courses and programs, and defined *curriculum* as academic plans. Kerr and Tweedy developed a curriculum model for learning outside the classroom that focused specifically on residence halls on campus (Kerr & Tweedy, 2006; Kerr, Tweedy, Edwards, & Kimmel, 2017). I reject the false dichotomy of curricular and cocurricular that establishes an assumption that some forms of learning are better than others—learning involves all the curriculum. Therefore, I use the word *curriculum* broadly to apply to a variety of contexts, including a major, a single course, programming for a student organization, or an experience as a member of an athletic team. For example, I serve as the faculty adviser for a fraternity, and we have a member development plan, which is a curriculum for the organization.

Kerr et al. (2017) reported substantial positive changes because of their curriculum model approach to education, including increased student participation in residential programming because administrators can explain to students the expected learning outcomes of participating. They also noted

> significant reductions in campus conduct interventions (regularly 30% and even as high as 50% reductions) in the first year of implementation as a result of reframing and better articulating what it means to be in a community guided by learning. (p. 26)

In its first decade, the curriculum model evolved to serve a broader mission across student affairs rather than being limited to residence life. In describing this shift, Kerr et al. (2017) called for the term *educator* to be applied outside the classroom:

> If all of our student life staff members and other out-of-the-classroom colleagues view themselves as educators and can readily quantify the value of educational opportunities and demonstrate related results, we will fare well when faced with questions about return on investment, contributions to learning, and other measures of value within and external to the academy. (pp. 29–30)

This represents great progress, but more work is ahead. It is not enough for out-of-the-classroom colleagues to view themselves as educators; faculty, parents, and students need to acknowledge that these professionals are educators as well. In building a curriculum to promote integration of learning, we must view one another as partners rather than strangers, or worse, adversaries.

Kerr et al. (2017) also wrote about the importance of quality in designing educational experiences, stating that their curriculum model is intentional in designing learning experiences for students outside the formal classroom environment and "holds those experiences beyond the classroom, and their facilitation, to the same expectations of pedagogical design as any learning endeavor on a college campus" (p. 22).

In the spirit of a rigorous curriculum model, this chapter brings together the practices from the preceding five chapters in a planning matrix mapping the three approaches to integration of learning onto the five practices described in this book. This is a practical resource that educators can use in their own curriculum development. I keep track of this curriculum development using a matrix I created, which is shown in Table 9.1. Table 9.2 is a blank matrix that you may use as a worksheet for your own planning.

I encourage you to begin by indicating which approaches to integration of learning (connection, application, and synthesis) your class activities prompt students to use. You may want to make copies of this matrix so you can write on it and mark it up for different courses and activities over time.

TABLE 9.1
Integration of Learning Planning Matrix: Student Experience by Practice and Integrative Approach

Practice	Connection	Application	Synthesis
Mentoring students	Students have a point of contact with a mentor who expresses interest in them and their work.	Students have a mentor who engages in a more in-depth dialogue about how ideas or knowledge from one context helps them to see in another.	Students have an ongoing relationship with a mentor who helps to make meaning about their experiences and helps them to see how multiple experiences and knowledge from disparate spheres comes together for the student.
Writing as praxis	Students search similarities in ideas through writing. Writing is a process to search for relationships.	Students use writing formulas or a framework learned in one context and apply it in another. At first, this can look like mimicking another author's work. It is hoped that somewhere between plagiarism and making it one's own, there is a place for modeling and imitation: "This is how to do it."?	Students bring together disparate ideas into a new narrative. This is a creative process, sometimes abstract in nature.

(Continues)

TABLE 9.1 (Continued)

Practice	Connection	Application	Synthesis
Encourage juxtaposition	Students compare and contrast ideas that are placed next to one another and recognize interesting differences.	Students actively wrestle with how disparate, perhaps conflicting, ideas can coexist.	Students find ways to reconcile juxtaposed ideas into a new way of seeing the knowledge and perhaps the world.
Hands-on experiences	Students have an idea that knowledge can be used in the world and an initial awareness that lessons learned in principle can be enacted in real life.	Students put learned knowledge and skills into action. They realize they have agency to do something that brings an idea into the real world. They have a sense of the ability to act but are not yet entirely comfortable or confident.	Students can choose knowledge and skills appropriate to a changing situation. They have a sense of independence in their own abilities and can modify and combine learning from multiple contexts to meet the demands of the situation at hand.
Embrace diversity and identity	Students have initial exposure to others who have different identities and backgrounds; students are comfortable bringing their unique identity and previous experience into the educational environment. Students possess a general awareness that multiple perspectives exist.	Students can use lenses from an identity that is not their own to look at information, a problem, or an issue. Students can use knowledge of multiple perspectives to build social and working relationships with others who are different from themselves.	Students can bring together their own identity with the perspectives they have learned from diverse others; aspects of personal identity are changed as a consequence of interaction with diverse others.

TABLE 9.2
Blank Integration of Learning Planning Matrix

Practice	Connection	Application	Synthesis
Mentoring students			
Writing as praxis			
Encourage juxtaposition			
Hands-on experiences			
Embrace diversity and identity			

Circle, check, or otherwise indicate those boxes for yourself. For example, in creating assignments and educational experiences for my students, I try to include a connection, an application, and a synthesis to meet the varied needs of students who make meaning and integrate learning in different ways. I also include at least three of the five practices in my course or program curriculum at least once. When you reflect on your own practice and indicate on the matrix which approaches your assignments and activities prompt for students, you create a visual of what kids of integration your course expects of students. The matrix is not a formula (e.g., if you check all the boxes, your students will integrate learning); rather it is a self-assessment and planning tool that provides a clear visual of where strengths lie and where gaps exist in your work regarding the integration of learning model.

Addressing the Needs of Disparate Learners

Now that we have examined these five practices in depth, it is time to put them into action. One of the most formidable challenges in working with a college student population is the range of experiences and meaning-making that can exist in any given group. Courses, student organizations, or residential environments likely include a range of traditional-age students between 18 and 22 years old, as well as non-traditional-age students. All of them have a diverse set of life experiences and are at a variety of locations along the meaning-making continuum, from externally driven to entering self-authorship. The broad range of characteristics in a group of college students not only keeps our work as college educators new and exciting but also poses a challenge in how to create a curriculum that is meaningful to individuals who see the world in very different ways.

Table 9.1 and the accompanying blank matrix worksheet in Table 9.2 serve as tools for college educators to visualize how well their curriculum focuses on integration of learning and how the curriculum may be experienced by a range of learners. The goal is to tailor your experience for the unique group of students you have at that time, knowing that this composition will change from semester to semester even if the course or organization remains consistent. For example, an experience that focuses heavily on synthesis in writing may be an amazing learning activity for a student with a great deal of previous writing experience and a complex meaning-making orientation, but it may be frustrating for a student with less practice writing and a less complex way of seeing the world; perhaps this student would be better reached by an assignment that focused more on connection through a juxtaposition of ideas. Creating a curriculum that includes multiple approaches to promoting integration of learning will better serve a diverse group of students.

This approach is not just about mastery of the material; we expect for students in a particular course or group to meet the learning outcomes of the experience. The focus of this book is helping students integrate what they are learning into their larger worldview and knowledge base. Offering a variety of ways for students to approach this integration provides a better chance for success in integration of learning.

The Integrative Lens

Above all else, I strive to introduce students to a mind-set of integration. I want them to view their world with an integrative lens, always looking for how things are connected, applying what they already know to new situations and problems, and synthesizing knowledge and skills to create new ways of seeing their experience. The college curriculum is important, and certainly I want to see students integrate on campus, but in the bigger picture I want them to start thinking in integrative ways and seeking opportunities to integrate learning outside my class or experience, beyond college, and into their lives beyond graduation.

Integration of learning is a habit of mind that builds on itself. Once you see integration of learning, it's hard to unsee it. The integrative lens becomes a part of your worldview. The college experience, and life in general, is no longer a series of discrete courses and compartmentalized experiences. It is a way of looking at the world as interconnected learning experiences.

Ideally your students will reach a point where they are always searching for ways to connect their learning. They go beyond thinking about what they learned in a specific course and consider how what they learned most recently fits with, complements, contradicts, or enhances what they already know. They think about how what they learned in one context fits with what they have learned in other perhaps very different contexts.

This is the integrative lens. When I design a curriculum inside and outside the classroom, I am thinking with an integrative lens. How does this content connect with what students have learned in other contexts? How will I get students to think about and acknowledge these connections? How does this course link to other courses the student is taking? How does it connect with their other learning experiences in student organizations, work, internships?

Before we can instill this integrative lens for students, we must adopt it ourselves. We can't look at the work we are doing in isolation, regardless of our role on campus. As faculty, staff, and student affairs administrators, we must ask ourselves how the learning experiences we provide for students interface with other learning experiences in which they are engaged both on and off campus. Whether you are a faculty member, a residence hall director, an athletic coach, or an internship supervisor, the work you are doing with students needs to be integrative and explicitly take into account the other contexts where students are learning.

University campuses are a collection of silos. Disciplines, majors, student organizations, academic affairs and student affairs, and residence halls are all distinct cultures with their own jargon, rituals, expectations, and learning outcomes. Students are involved in several of these silos from day one and are often the primary connectors between those silos. Administrators, faculty, and staff work mainly within their specific silo but students come and go among several silos every day. Students in the Wabash National Study of Liberal Arts Education (Barber 2009, 2012) did not often talk about faculty or staff support or involvement in terms of integration of learning. Instead, they were integrating on their own with the help of peers.

As educators and colleagues, we need to conceptualize an intercontextual curriculum. We need to go outside our silos and actively help students integrate learning across contexts.

Conceptualizing an Intercontextual Curriculum

These are fancy words, but at the core, this is about broadening the view of a college curriculum to not only include life experiences beyond the campus but also seek and embrace them and help students use them to learn concepts in the classroom. These life experiences are often not even acknowledged let alone embraced. Internships, residence life, intercollegiate athletics, study abroad and study away, organization membership, and work study are all opportunities for student learning in the college context. To promote integration of learning broadly, we must consider a full range of educational experiences that are a part of students' collegiate years and extend beyond the classroom and campus. I discuss the various outcomes of these experiences next.

Disciplinary Curriculum Outcomes

At a basic level we tend to think of college learning outcomes as major specific. An English major will learn certain content that is different from what a chemistry major learns. Each major or discipline is a silo where a defined set of knowledge and skills are mastered. These outcomes are intended to provide knowledge and skills for a particular job or field, and monetary wealth and career earnings are some of the important factors that measure how well someone is doing professionally.

Cross-Disciplinary Perspectives and Outcomes

In addition to the discipline-specific expectations for learning outcomes, those that cut across disciplines are outcomes we expect students to have at graduation regardless of their major. The disciplines themselves are still siloed, but a group of learning outcomes that cuts across all of them are skills that include written and oral communication, quantitative reasoning, and working with diverse others. National organizations such as the AAC&U have various lists of these overarching outcomes, and there is a great degree of agreement on what these outcomes should be. Through its Liberal Education and America's Progress program, the AAC&U (n.d.) identified four broad categories of essential learning outcomes: knowledge of human cultures and the physical and natural world, intellectual and practical skills, personal and social responsibility, and integrative and applied learning.

Cocurricular Outcomes

On this next level, campus experiences outside the formal curriculum are added to the educational map. The formal curriculum remains a silo from this vantage point alongside other collegiate learning experiences such as residence life, student organizations, and internships. The context for learning is still limited to the university campus, but experiences outside for-credit courses are included and valued. The cocurricular outcomes are developed across many experiences in the college environment, inside and outside the traditional classroom. Thus, the definition of *college educators* includes student affairs professionals, administrators, athletic coaches and staff, and organization advisers, in addition to faculty members.

Intercontextual Outcomes

This view of learning goes a step further to embrace learning experiences that happen totally outside the college campus but still have an impact as they create learning that is integrated with campus experiences and ideas. Outcomes cut across not only the campus contexts inside and outside the classroom but also other significant life experiences such as work, family, faith or worldview involvement, and living situations. This view is intercontextual in that we conceptualize learning as happening and prompting connections across all the varied contexts that a student encounters during the college years, and formal class experiences are just a fraction of these contexts.

Developmental Considerations

Opportunities for challenge and support should be embedded in the curriculum. We want students to be supported in their excitement about what they are learning and see they can not only integrate learning across contexts but also be challenged to see things in new ways and make connections that may be uncomfortable at first. Building a curriculum that does this is complicated by the fact that we are not working with a developmentally homogenous group of undergraduate students. Even in a course or program focused on a single group of students, such as a first-year writing course, there is a range of meaning-making and integrative ability in that group. Some students may still be firmly entrenched in external frameworks, waiting for authorities to tell them where connections lie while they are sitting next to a student who is moving through the crossroads into more internal foundations. This scenario is complicated further when considering that most courses, student organizations, or experiential leaning activities like study abroad host undergraduates from several classes, perhaps first-year through senior, representing a broader range of ages from 17 to 23 and older and varied meaning-making positions.

We need to acknowledge this diversity in our students and incorporate opportunities at a variety of levels for students to find challenge and support in our curricula. Several tools can help us facilitate integration of learning for students.

Practical Strategies for Educators

In this section, I offer several ways to approach the task of creating a curriculum to promote integration of learning for college students.

Menu Approach

A menu approach provides the flexibility to allow students to choose their own assignments to demonstrate their learning. Create a selection (your menu) of five to six assignments that help students meet the outcomes of the course, and let them choose which two to three assignments they want to complete. Make sure they are aware of deadlines, and establish clear expectations for when work is due so you can provide timely feedback. However, beware the logistical challenges of this strategy. I have found myself in trouble with this option in the past when I let students choose from a menu of assignments and also choose when in the semester they would submit the work. Everyone in the class had a different time frame, resulting in a slow drip of work coming in rather than a defined due date and grading time for me. I quickly lost track of what was coming in when and ended up with a backlog of different assignments to grade. Sometimes I was unable to provide feedback on one assignment before the student turned in the next. Therefore, I would recommend identifying specific dates when assignments are due, regardless of which assignments students choose to complete.

Self-Designed Assignments

Challenge students to devise their own assignment that will (a) demonstrate mastery of the content area and (b) explicitly draw on learning from another context or connect to another area of their life. This allows students to choose the format of the work and conceptualize how it relates to the class and their lives. As students create their own assignments, they must also come up with how it will be graded or otherwise assessed. Is there a rubric? What constitutes acceptable or excellent work? I have found that when given this opportunity to choose their own adventure, students usually do an excellent job, come up with ideas that are way more creative than what I had in mind, and are more excited about the assignments. I have also found that they are harder on themselves than I would be. They tend to make the projects longer and more complex and also set the bar higher for assessment. To mitigate this, I usually have students draft a proposed plan, and then I can review it and offer suggestions to be sure they are not overdoing it.

Transparency

Be clear with students about your strategy: You've put a great deal of time into planning your curriculum with resources, assignments, exercises, and field trips. Be transparent with students about how you have organized the experience for them and why. Demonstrate the variety of approaches you have included, and encourage them to find ways to use their strengths and try new ways of thinking, learning, and integrating that may not be in their repertoire yet. In a course context, you could even add this information to the syllabus, that is, showing them how each assignment relates to other contexts and prompts integration of learning.

Scaffolding in the Curriculum

In your curriculum, build up to more complex integration. Start with simple connections. Ask students to relate ideas from the course to their lives, then add application in which you ask students to use knowledge or skills leaned in one context in a new way. Next, move to synthesis, prompting students to bring ideas from different places together to form something new. Remember, as students become more complex thinkers, they use all three kinds of integration in concert, so build up to assignments or tasks that incorporate connection, application, and synthesis.

Experiment and Innovate

Try new things as an educator. In building a curriculum, it's necessary to be deliberate and measured about what knowledge you expect students to gain from the experience. However, curriculum design is also a creative process that requires some degree of experimentation. We have to be willing to experiment to try new approaches to teaching and learning to keep our students and ourselves engaged. New technologies, innovations, and a changing political and social landscape require continuous revisions to a curriculum. Learning experiences developed even two years ago can seem dated. Cultural references and examples have an even shorter shelf life. The undergraduate population is always in flux; each year the senior class graduates and moves on from the institution, and a new group of first-year students matriculates. Every four to five years, we have a complete turnover of undergraduates, often with experiences and expectations quite different from those of their predecessors.

Capstone Experiences and Signature Work

How are you helping students see the bigger picture? How are you helping them put it all together? What is the capstone or culminating experience for your class or program? Ideally, capstone experiences are not the only integrative aspect of a curriculum. You don't want to have several siloed (compartmentalized) experiences and then a final capstone as the culminating experience. We need to scaffold this skill and start prompting integrated learning from our early interactions with students. You don't promote integration of learning by simply adding a capstone experience at the end of a course, major, or program. You need to build up to that capstone from step one. To build a truly integrative curriculum, you need to integrate learning the whole way through.

Senior capstone experiences are intentionally integrative learning experiences. Overall, integration of learning can be an outcome of senior capstone experiences and is an overarching goal of senior year experiences in general (Cuseo, 1998). The AAC&U (2017) broadened this concept of capstones to include signature work experiences that encourage students to integrate and apply their learning to complex problems and projects that are important to the individual student and the greater community and society. Research suggests that the use of a constructive developmental pedagogy is particularly effective for promoting self-authorship and integration of learning (Baxter Magolda, 1999; Baxter Magolda & King, 2004; Boes, 2006; Kegan, 1994). Like most educational interventions, senior capstone experiences can be well designed and implemented or poorly so. The design and implementation of this experience, more so than the format (course, project, thesis) or the content (discipline based, interdisciplinary, cocurricular) determines how effective it will be in promoting the integration of learning for undergraduate college students. There is more than one route to integration of learning, and senior capstone experiences are certainly one pathway that can be effective with the proper tools.

No matter what combination of strategies and activities are implemented, creating an integration-focused curriculum takes time and can take place on many different levels. You can start with a course, program, or activity that you are responsible for and are leading. Start by thinking about the big picture: How can this experience help my students integrate their learning?

Summary

Once we build a curriculum for our students, we must figure out how to determine if it is working. How do we know students' educational experiences result in learning? How do we know students are integrating learning? In addition to creating the educational experiences, we also need to assess the experiences. Assessment will show us how students are learning and help us improve the curriculum to make it even better. We also need to document students' learning to communicate the outcomes to a range of stakeholders, fellow educators, administrators, accreditation teams, policymakers, family members, and the students themselves.

For the most part, our assessment methods in higher education focus on compartmentalization. Exams or research papers cover material from a section of a course (midterms) or a semester-long course (finals). Grades are given for a specific course, which is meant to evaluate, illustrate, or demonstrate mastery of the content of that course. There are exceptions such as capstone projects intended to bring together an entire major or discipline and comprehensive exams (usually at the graduate level) that focus on integration. However, these are the exceptions and not the rule. In general, our methods for assessing student learning focus on compartmentalizing learning rather than integrating it. In the next chapter, I provide several techniques for assessing and documenting integration of learning.

Reflection Questions: Things to Think About in Your Educational Practice

Take a few minutes to read and reflect on the following questions. Jot down your thoughts on paper, your phone, your laptop, or wherever is convenient. Be as formal or informal as you like in how you respond; the important thing is that you give yourself time to reflect.

1. Consider the big picture. How does this course, program, or activity help your students to integrate their learning?
2. How do you incorporate multiple strategies for integration in your work with students? This is the vertical part of the matrix, include as many of the five practices as possible.
3. How do you address the needs of students at different levels in your work? This is the horizontal part of the matrix, include opportunities for connecting, applying, and synthesizing.
4. How do you link my course or program to other aspects of students' lives, through colleagues at your institution?
5. How do you promote the integrative lens for your students?

10

DOCUMENTING AND ASSESSING INTEGRATION OF LEARNING

How do you know that students can integrate learning? As we look to promote integration of learning for students through our work as college educators, the point is not to create these integrative experiences as one-offs but rather to teach students how to integrate learning so they can do it throughout their lives. The five practices presented in this book teach and model the process for students, but it is important for educators to be able to document and assess students' learning to provide feedback to students, demonstrate students' mastery of the outcomes, maintain accreditation, and secure funding and human resources. Assessment techniques discussed in this chapter include individual interviews, focus groups, observations, cocurricular transcripts, rubrics, quantitative scales, and portfolios.

Assessment has a bad reputation. In some higher education circles, the mere mention of the *A* word sends people running for the door. To many, assessment has become conflated with administrative bloat and academic bureaucracy. This contributes to a false narrative that assessment exists for the sole purpose of satisfying accrediting agencies every 5 or 10 years.

Indeed, assessment is not just for administrators and accreditation. Assessment is a process to find out if you're meeting your goals for student learning and whether or not students are achieving what you want them to. Assessment often gets a bad rap as extra work primarily for accreditors' use, but in reality, assessment is simply a plan for documenting and communicating student learning.

According to Jodi Fisler, associate for assessment policy and analysis at the State Council of Higher Education for Virginia, "Assessment is evidence-based storytelling" (J. Fisler, personal communication, February 6, 2018).

How do students bring together their work as evidence to tell the story of how they are connecting learning? How are they integrating learning?

As educational leaders, we must be aware of the different paradigms in play, such as the instruction paradigm, which focuses on the teacher, and the learning paradigm, which places the student at the center (Barr & Tagg, 1995). We must intentionally design our assessment to promote the learning we desire. If we truly want to promote integrated learning for college students, then we must create modes of assessment that value it. Standardized tests alone do not adequately capture the complex thinking required of integration. We must develop assessment strategies that reveal and document meaning-making over time. More so, we must create a strong evidence-based culture that provides clear directions for college educators on how to assess and document student learning (Bingham, Bureau, & Duncan, 2015). In other words, we assess what we value.

Assessment Cycle

Assessment is often described as a cyclical process, but often the cycle is left incomplete. The most commonly skipped step in the cycle is using the data collected to make improvements. Ideally, educators take what they find through assessment and use that information to improve the learning environment, curriculum, and outcomes to be better for the next iteration. No course, experience, or assignment is perfect because there are always elements that can be improved in the next go-round.

The assessment cycle is a four-step continuous process: establish learning goals, provide learning opportunities, assess student learning, and use the results (Suskie, 2018). I have modified these steps to relate directly to integration of learning among college students (see Figure 10.1). Next, I describe the four steps in my modified integration of learning assessment cycle.

Establish Integrative Learning Goals

Intentionally place integration of learning as one of your learning outcomes for your class or program. Add it to your syllabus or to the remarks for your first meeting with students. I have learned to be direct and shameless about noting that I want students to learn how to link learning across contexts as a result of participating in my course, a study abroad program, or a student organization. For example, one of the learning outcomes of my first-year writing seminar is: "By the end of the term, students who are successful in this course will be able to integrate their learning in this course with prior knowledge, experience, and skills through the creation of written work." It

Figure 10.1. The integration of learning assessment cycle.

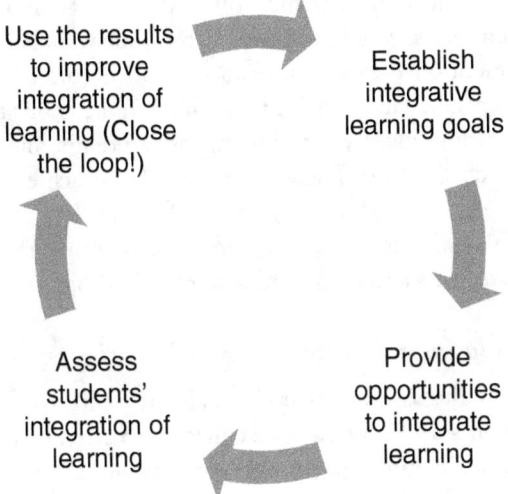

is clear, it's in the syllabus, and we talk about what that means on day one. If you don't set out to promote integration of learning from the start, it may happen for students but it will be more by luck than by design.

Provide Opportunities to Integrate Learning

Once you have established that integration of learning is an outcome of your educational experience you want students to demonstrate, then you must provide opportunities for them to integrate learning. As discussed in chapter 9, you need to create a curriculum to promote integration of learning. This step in the cycle is the focus of much of this book. College educators should include opportunities for mentoring; incorporate varied forms of writing; juxtapose disparate ideas, skills, and environments; create opportunities for hands-on learning; and emphasize diversity and identity in their work with students. This is the fun part: building interesting, creative experiences that will scaffold student learning and guide them toward integration of learning.

Assess Students' Integration of Learning

How do you know the students have integrated learning? This question echoes in my mind as I think about student learning. How do I know they can connect, apply, and synthesize learning across contexts? If I know they have integrated learning, how can I document this learning in a way I can easily show others? How can I communicate this achievement to the various stakeholders, the fellow educators, parents, policymakers, accreditation teams, and the students themselves, which may require multiple ways of communicating the results. As mentioned earlier, assessment is at its core a process of documenting and communicating student learning. Figuring out the best way to answer these questions given your context, your students, and your role as an educator can be challenging. There is no formula as each experience will be different, but there is no shortage of options for you. Later in this chapter I provide several techniques or strategies and assessing integration of learning among college students and communicating the findings.

Use the Results to Improve Integration of Learning

This final step in the assessment cycle is also the most often forgotten or ignored. Too often assessment data are collected to checkboxes, submit final grades for a course, include with budget requests, attach with grant applications or satisfy accreditation requirements. The assessment is completed, data are compiled, and then the report sits on a shelf or is more likely stored somewhere in the cloud never to be seen again. This common behavior misses one of the most important reasons for assessment: to improve student learning. You must close the loop and link the fourth step in the cycle (using the results) to the first step (establishing integrative learning goals) and start the assessment cycle over again. How can you use the results of your assessment efforts to revise your learning goals for your course or program? What will you do to improve your work with students based on the results? Every educational experience has room for improvement. Close the loop, and use the results to better promote integration of learning.

Assessment speaks volumes about our values. We assess what we value, so if we truly value integration of learning, we must put resources into assessing it. The longitudinal interviews from the Wabash National Study of Liberal Arts Education (Baxter Magolda & King, 2007, 2012) allowed follow-up questions to probe deeper into students' meaning-making. Interviewers held conversations with students over the course of four years to get a picture of how students connected, applied, and synthesized learning over their college career and, more broadly, how they experienced a liberal arts education. The narrative that emerged over four years was quite different from what was captured at any one point in time.

There is also an important distinction to consider between research and assessment. The work of the Wabash National Study was research, systematically collecting and analyzing data to inform and advance theories of liberal arts education. With a goal of understanding students' experience and improving learning, assessment may be on a smaller scale than the national scope of the Wabash National Study. An assessment process might focus on a single program, classroom, or student to garner data to help students integrate learning. Research studies like the Wabash National Study are necessary and vital to advance our knowledge about college student learning, but they are not the only method to assess integration of learning. You do not have to launch a 4-year longitudinal study to assess and document integration of learning.

The Importance of Communication About Assessment Across Contexts

To get a sense of assessing integration of learning for students, in addition to talking with students themselves, it is also relevant to talk with others engaged in assessment across your institution. Specialized assessment professionals are increasingly common in higher education. For example, an assessment professional may be in the provost's office and another in student affairs, and other faculty or staff may be working on assessment or accreditation in an institution's departments and schools. How often do these assessment experts come together to share data, align methods and calendars, and discuss integration of learning across the institution? Coordination varies greatly by institution. A few institutions may have well established lines of communication across areas, but most have limited cooperation across the organizational chart. Creating opportunities for communication about assessment across the institution should become a priority.

Approaches to Assessment for Integration of Learning

In this section, I offer several methods for assessing and documenting integration of learning among college students. In keeping with the spirit of intercontextual curricula, these approaches are not classroom bound. They can be used in the context of a traditional academic course, but they are flexible and can be applied broadly across college experiences.

Interviews and Focus Groups

Individual interviews and focus groups can provide firsthand information about how students integrate learning. Sitting down with students for a conversation about their learning can serve multiple purposes. It acts as a means of data collection for documenting the learning experiences students have and how they are making meaning of them, and it also can be an intervention to help students reflect and consider the ways that what they are learning are resulting in an aha moment or integration in situ.

The Wabash National Study (Baxter Magolda & King, 2012) interviews were effective and productive because they were in depth (60–90 minutes), and semistructured. Interviewers encouraged students to cocreate the interviews, and the format allowed the interviewer to probe further with follow-up questions to elicit meaning-making. How the student answered a particular question mapped the course of the interview just as much as the framework of possible questions that made up the interview protocol.

Conversations about student learning through interviews or focus groups are excellent methods for assessing integration of learning because they allow immediate follow up and probing by the interviewer. When a student mentions an experience that led to integration, the interviewer can ask additional questions to clarify and gain more information about the practices and conditions. This approach elicits details of students' perceptions and meaning-making and their process for integrating, which are difficult to capture using any other method. However, conducting interviews and focus groups is time consuming and difficult to scale, especially with limited resources. Because of this, interviews and focus groups are more common for research involving small populations of students.

Inclusive Transcripts

Cocurricular or experiential transcripts are a practical way to show that learning is not restricted to the classroom or the formal curriculum. Students and graduates may capture the breadth of their experiences on their résumés if they are shown how to do so.

The American Association of Collegiate Registrars and Admissions Officers and the National Association of Student Personnel Administrators, with funding from the Lumina Foundation, have developed models for comprehensive student records that capture learning (Lumina Foundation, 2016). These records are, in essence, a detailed transcript of learning experiences outside the traditional course-based curriculum and may include residence life, commuter and dual-enrollment student life, and military service. Using these models, student activities, leadership roles, and internship experiences can be documented in a way that is easy for future employers to see the extent of experiential learning alongside the academic records, letter grades, and grade point average of a traditional transcript. According to the Lumina Foundation (2016),

> Learning occurs in many different ways and places, both day and night. The comprehensive student record project supported the innovative work

of colleges and universities that tried new ways of verifying and documenting the diverse experiences of today's learners that help them hone and develop knowledge, skills, and abilities. This convening will showcase the efforts of the participating institutions, what they learned, and what these results mean for capturing all learning, regardless of how and where it happens. (para. 1)

Evergreen State College uses narrative evaluations of courses rather than letter grades. Faculty members write a detailed account of each student's work and progress in the course, which is then paired with the student's self-evaluation. According to Evergreen State College (n.d.), "Narrative evaluations express the thinking that went into your work, what you completed, and the reactions of both you and your faculty members to your work. These detailed documents often provide specific examples of achievement or progress" (para. 1). The narratives for each course are then compiled into a comprehensive transcript of the student's work at the institution. A narrative format could easily be modified to specifically address integration of learning across the formal curriculum and educational experiences including study abroad, service-learning, student leadership, internships, and residence life.

Portfolios

Portfolios are another excellent means of documenting student learning and have the added advantage of capturing student reflection and illustrating how students are integrating learning. Although holistic transcripts and comprehensive student records can show a fuller picture of what students did in college, portfolios allow students to show how they make meaning of those disparate experiences and connect them across contexts.

Comprehensive or cocurricular transcripts are a much needed tool in the documentation process, but to really determine students' integration, you need students' reflections (see chapter 3) as well as strong feedback for the student. The process of building a portfolio is not as meaningful if it is merely a series of checkboxes for students to complete before graduation and lacks feedback from the educators they know. The relationship matters. Feedback on a portfolio from your adviser, or another mentor, will have a greater impact than feedback from an anonymous reviewer or no feedback at all.

Portfolios are evidence of student learning. They cannot capture every aspect of learning, but they can represent aspects of integration for others to see. Like any form of documentation, it is a snapshot of the ways the students were thinking at the time the portfolio was created. It is representative of their capacity for integration of learning at that time. This book about integration of learning is different from my dissertation and previous writing on the subject. My future work on integration of learning will also be different because I will be a different thinker in the future as my meaning-making continues to develop, and therefore I will see the world and integration of learning differently as time marches on.

Reynolds and Patton (2014) described their process for constructing an ePortfolio system in terms of three uses: for faculty's classes or projects, for programs or institution-wide use, and for tenure and promotion portfolios. They noted that the portfolio itself is a vehicle for documenting and communicating learning, but the portfolio itself needs to be assessed: "If you are going to do the work necessary to change your practice [to promote integrative learning], then knowing if those changes actually give you the results you want is critical" (p. 148).

Formative and Summative Feedback

A portfolio or any other form of documentation or assessment is a snapshot of an ongoing learning process. Thus the feedback we provide should be summative and formative. Summative feedback is evaluative and typically given at the end of a course or program to show how well a student achieved the learning outcomes or goals of the experience. Formative feedback, however, is intended to help students improve their work and is generally provided during the process, perhaps on a draft of an assignment. It's not intended to be evaluative but rather to help move the work forward, so it might include comments or a critique without a grade attached. For a structured academic course, you generally need to assign a final grade. If you are using an ePortfolio as a culminating project, you need to evaluate that work and give a grade based on whatever rubric or criteria you have established for and with students. That final grade is summative, that is, it sums up the student's effort on that project. However, because integration of learning is an ongoing process, it would be helpful to also provide formative feedback on the process, not the portfolio or product per se but the ways the student is thinking, integrating, and describing the learning.

A challenge in providing useful feedback that is summative and formative is getting students to read it. I know from experience that undergraduates often look for that final grade—the summative evaluation—and don't go any further. They flip or scroll through the pages to the end to see what the final grade is without reading any of your comments. Or worse, they log in to the course management system to see how many points they got and never return to the original work or your comments. If there is a way for you to incorporate a brief meeting or conference with students to discuss their portfolio, do it. Using this method, you can provide formative and summative feedback directly to the student and also ask the student follow-up questions about their work and learning. This ties to the discussion in chapter 4 on mentoring and building a rapport with students. Even a 10-minute meeting provides a chance for you to present feedback to students that they can learn from, build on, and ideally integrate into future learning experiences inside and outside traditional college settings.

Sometimes the grading process can be an obstacle to integrating learning. The focus from the educator's perspective is on evaluating the product the student submits, grading the exam, or adding up the points for a final grade. This is often a solitary (siloed) and monotonous process, performed at the hectic end of the term and with the registrar's scheduled deadline. For students grading can also be perceived as compartmentalized. What matters most to many students is the final letter grade, the summative evaluation for the course that will appear on their transcript and factor into their grade point average. The comments from the instructor simply do not factor in, despite the level of care and time a faculty member puts into writing the comments (I know that for faculty members this is hard to read).

For educational experiences that are not graded, like an internship or a leadership position, students may not get any assessment, summative or formative, unless they ask for it from an educator involved with the program. Initiating a simple rule of creating conversations with students about what they are learning and finding the best way to document the feedback (in both directions) from those experiences is of the utmost importance. We must develop better ways of assessing and documenting the broad scope of student learning in addition to, or eventually in place of, the grading system that was first developed in the eighteenth century, which was a very different time in higher education.

Millner (2018) described how he changed his approach to grading essays by not writing on his students' papers at all. Instead, he invited students to meet with him individually to discuss their work and their grades. His experiment paid off and brought a renewed sense of passion to his teaching and a new dynamic to his interactions with students. He concluded with a remark that aligns perfectly with the notion of integration of learning:

> I came to have a better sense of my students' lives and experiences and how all of that might connect with the work we do in the classroom. I didn't blame them anymore for quickly glancing at the grade on their papers and skimming my comments. They were making a point about this way of communicating, which was on a perfect continuum with their worlds of work schedules and bureaucratic managers. (para. 26)

Millner found a way to mentor each student and learn more about their identities and how their lives connected with what they were studying in class. He had conversations with students, which better aligned with their learning experiences outside his class in their work and internships.

Quantitative Scale

In Barber et al. (2017), we created a factor consisting of three survey items to document integration of learning: the extent to which students believed their courses helped them "see connections between their intended career and how it affects society," their out-of-class experiences helped them "connect what was learned in the classroom with life events," and their out-of-class experiences helped them "translate knowledge and understanding from the classroom into action" (p. 7).

We performed exploratory factor analysis that is validated and reliable if used with a large sample and supports the qualitative findings from the Wabash National Study (Barber 2009, 2012, 2014) in relation to integration of learning. Although the longitudinal qualitative interviews we conducted for the Wabash National Study provided rich detail and invaluable insight into students' meaning-making processes, they are not the only way to assess integration of learning. Quantitative measures of integration of learning are possible and useful but do not allow the same type of probing and follow-up questioning that semistructured, longitudinal interviews with students provide.

Rubrics

Rubrics are tools for students and educators. For educators, they help in planning curricula and figuring out how the various experiences, assignments, or products in a course or organization help students meet the expected learning goals. For students, they help in making the expectations for success clear. So how can you build a rubric for integration of learning?

Table 9.1 in the previous chapter is one form of a rubric more specific to educators. It can help you plan your curriculum, including experiences inside and outside the classroom, and see if there are any gaps in practices to promote integration as well as approaches that will resonate with students at a variety of different meaning-making levels.

Another easy way to incorporate integration of learning into your rubrics is to make it a separate heading or row on your rubric, just as you might have for writing, argument, and so on. Table 10.1 is an example of a row you could incorporate into an established rubric.

Temporal Lag

It is also difficult to capture the scope of integration of learning in a portfolio or other method because there is no end point on integration of

TABLE 10.1
Sample Rubric for Integration of Learning

	A (Expert)	B (Intermediate)	C (Novice)
Integration of Learning	Student makes meaningful learning links across contexts using all three approaches to integration of learning: connection, application, and synthesis. Student has clearly reflected on own learning and can communicate how they are integrating.	Student has some ability to integrate learning but is largely restricted to connection and application; there is little complex synthesis. Student has some reflective skill but sometimes misses opportunities to integrate learning or has difficulty identifying links across contexts.	Student has minimal integration of learning and sees knowledge and skills as largely context bound. Student lacks reflection skills and cannot identify how learning may be integrated across contexts.

learning. Integration takes time, and there is often a temporal lag between when a learning experience happens and when students integrate learning (Barber et al., 2014). Although college graduation is a significant milestone, it is not the conclusion of learning and development, which continue throughout life. We don't walk across the stage and declare, "All the learning has been integrated, my work is done!" No, we continue to evolve as learners; we integrate new information we learn each day with what we already know, and often this newly integrated knowledge changes the way we make sense of the previous information. Even years later, I still look back on learning from my undergraduate experience and have new insights, such as "Aha! I didn't realize this fit together in that way!" or "Now I see what the professor was talking about in class, or why they loved this book so much."

Unfortunately, we don't always get to see this integration as a college student. Those light bulb moments often happen after the semester has ended, or once a student is in a first job. It's not captured in the student's final portfolio, and it isn't noted in your end-of-semester teaching evaluations because it hasn't happened yet.

As a side note, the next time you have one of these light bulb moments where you integrate learning and suddenly see the work of your college educators, faculty, or staff, in a new way, let them know! Send a quick email to thank them for laying that foundation for you years ago and to let them know that you appreciate their work. Even if your note is out of the blue, I guarantee it will be appreciated.

Summary

In thinking about assessment and documentation, we must see the experiences through the eyes of the students as well as the educators. It is important to find out where students make connections, not where you see them. Just because you designed an experience to be integrated or to promote integration does not mean students experience it that way; we need to find out how they view it.

In conclusion, integration of learning is about the process, not just the practice. There are myriad ways of prompting integration, but the habits of mind that sustain this type of learning are what's most important. It is essential for the next generation of college students to be skilled at integrating. Today's jobs, and certainly those of the future, require people to be able to take in vast amounts of information and make sense of it quickly using criteria and knowledge gained from previous experience. Graduates who cannot integrate learning well will be at a grave disadvantage. As college educators, we have an opportunity and a responsibility to equip our students with an integrative lens and the experiences to practice using it.

Reflection Questions: Things to Think About in Your Educational Practice

Take a few minutes to read and reflect on the following questions. Jot down your thoughts on paper, your phone, your laptop, or wherever is convenient. Be as formal or informal as you like in how you respond; the important thing is that you give yourself time to reflect.

1. How do you know that your students integrate learning?
2. How do you create a curriculum with assessment and documentation in mind?
3. How and when do you provide my students with formative feedback? With summative feedback?
4. Given that there is a temporal lag for integration of learning, how can you follow up after your program or course has ended to keep prompting students to integrate learning?
5. Who has prompted your own integration of learning, and how can you let them know of their impact?

APPENDIX A

Additional Details on Learning, Development, and Meaning for Those Who Care to Read It

Self-Authorship

Student development was of great interest to the Wabash National Study of Liberal Arts Education researchers, in particular because of the 4-year design of the study. However, this angle added a layer of complexity to our work. In addition to finding out what the undergraduates were learning (see the liberal arts outcomes in chapter 1), we also wanted to know how students were changing over the 4 years of the project. We used self-authorship (Baxter Magolda, 2004b, 2009; Kegan, 1994) as a framework for development. Kegan's model of human development proposed five orders of consciousness that unfold over the span of a person's life; self-authorship is the fourth order of consciousness. In his research, Kegan (1994) found that about one-third of adults in the United States were embedded in the third order of consciousness or somewhere between the third and fourth orders. Baxter Magolda focused on self-authorship (Kegan's Order 4) in her work with college students as higher education is uniquely positioned to help young adults make the transition from third order thinking to the more complex fourth order of consciousness. Kegan's model extends beyond self-authorship to self-transformation, the fifth order, achieved by only 1% of the population.

Self-authorship takes a constructive developmental view of personal growth. It is both constructivist, grounded in the belief that people construct their own meaning of the world around them, and developmental in that these ways of making meaning become more complex over time.

Meaning-Making

Meaning-making is a term I use often in this book to describe the complex ways that people make sense of the world around them, their own identities, and their relationships with others. Meaning-making suggests a holistic view of student development, concerned with the whole person rather than one particular area. Perry (1970) observed, "What organisms do is organize, and human organisms organize meaning" (p. 3). Baxter Magolda and King (2012) described meaning-making in higher education as follows:

> Applied to college student learning and development, meaning making refers to the strategies students use to understand what and how they are learning; each strategy provides the perspective that guides how they make meaning (not the content of their belief or decision). (p. 4)

The notion of meaning-making fits well with the constructive developmental frame advanced by self-authorship. It is an active, constructive process; individuals make meaning of their experiences as opposed to having the meaning provided to them. Similarly, meaning-making is a personal process; 10 students in a seminar may all experience the same events in a class discussion, and all 10 could make meaning of those events differently. Finally, meaning-making is developmental, and one's capacity for meaning-making grows more complex over time. The way a person makes meaning of an experience today is likely different from how the same person made meaning of the exact same experience two years prior. The way that we as individuals make meaning is developing all the time.

Dimensions of Development

In self-authorship theory, personal development occurs in three overlapping dimensions: cognitive, intrapersonal, and interpersonal (Baxter Magolda, 1999; Baxter Magolda & King, 2012; Kegan, 1994). The cognitive domain (also called the epistemological domain) focuses on how individuals see knowledge and the world around them. The intrapersonal domain focuses on a person's sense of self and identity. Finally, the interpersonal domain describes how people see their relationships.

Baxter Magolda (2004a) framed these three domains in terms of three crucial questions identified by traditional-age college students in their late teens and early 20s: "How do I know?" (cognitive), "Who am I?" (intrapersonal), and "How do I want to construct relationships with others?" (interpersonal). In examining these three dimensions of development, we look at personal growth holistically, concerned with the whole person rather than one area of that person's life. In the Wabash National Study, we have a keen interest in all these developmental domains, and each interview each year was assessed for meaning-making capacity in four areas: cognitive, intrapersonal, interpersonal, and overall. As a result, a student who participated in the study all 4 years as an undergraduate had a total of 16 self-authorship levels recorded, four each year, allowing us to track individual growth and change over the entire college career.

Phases of the Journey

Baxter Magolda described the growth over a person's lifetime in terms of a journey toward self-authorship. This journey is composed of 10 developmental positions along a continuum from external meaning-making to internal meaning-making. This continuum is divided into four main phases: external frameworks, entering crossroads, leaving crossroads, and early self-authorship.

People move from formulaic meaning-making, reliant on external frameworks and direction of authorities to transitional meaning-making, drawing on a mix of often conflicting external and internal influences. Transitional meaning-making, which Baxter Magolda (2004a) called "the Crossroads" (p. 93) is a challenging time when previous knowledge is contested and new ways of seeing the world are uncovered. People progress from transitional to foundational meaning-making, which is internally driven, drawing on established criteria and prior experience. It is important for educators to have a sense of how a student makes meaning because this knowledge can help create experiences that will challenge the student to make progress toward more internally driven meaning-making. See Table 2.2 for the 10 positions in the journey toward self-authorship.

Learning

As we consider the role of development in the process of integration, we must also consider theories of how people learn. For more than a century, educational researchers have studied the ways people transfer learning from one context to another. In chapter 1 I discuss the definitions related to integrative learning. Now I want to introduce briefly some of the research on human learning.

Ideas about the transferability of learning go back more than a century in educational research. Two classical theories are the foundation of the literature about learning transfer. The first is the idea of *general principles* by Charles Judd (1908, 1939), and the second is the concept of *identical elements* by Edward Thorndike (1924). Thorndike's work built on an earlier study (Thorndike & Woodworth, 1901) that examined the impact of learning in one context on learning in other contexts. That study failed to find much influence, and the researchers concluded that the ability to transfer learning depended not on learning general subjects like Latin or geometry but instead on the presence of identical elements in two situations.

Judd (1939) disagreed with Thorndike's (1924) theory of identical elements and suggested that understanding the general principles of subject matter was most important. This shift from focusing on discrete details to general principles sets the stage for a new way of thinking about teaching and learning that privileged conceptual learning over memorization. These foundational ideas are critical to the conceptualization of integration of learning as an educational outcome and paved the way for later theories about transfer of learning, which explore in more depth issues of how influential the environment is on individuals' cognition, meaning-making, and ability to transfer learning. However, there is a major disagreement between the classical theories of transfer and later cognitive and situated views of transfer. The central criticism of the classical theories is that they reinforce a separation of education from life, institutionally and epistemologically (Tuomi-Gröhn & Engeström, 2003).

Perkins and Salomon (1992) defined *transfer of learning* as occurring "when learning in one context or with one set of materials impacts on performance in another context or with other related materials" (p. 1). However, Larkin (1989) argued that transfer is more than simply applying old knowledge in new situations. She stated that transfer of learning is "applying old knowledge in a setting sufficiently novel that it also requires learning new knowledge" (p. 283).

APPENDIX B

Student Examples

Student	Institution	Gender	Race/Ethnicity*	Year	Practice	Chapter
Fran	Hudson	Female	White	1	Juxtaposition	1
Elliot	Wabash	Male	White	2	Hands-on	2
Colin	Wabash	Male	White, Hispanic	2	Juxtaposition	2
Nick	Greenleaf	Male	White	4	Juxtaposition	2
Ethan	Hudson	Male	White, Jewish	2	Writing	3
Gavin	St. Bernadette	Male	White	1	Writing	3
Kayla	Hudson	Female	Asian/Pacific Islander, Korean	2	Hands-On	3
Tyler	Wabash	Male	African American	2	Writing	5
Tyler	Wabash	Male	African American	5	Writing	5
Wallace	Wabash	Male	White	2	Writing	5
Matt	Wabash	Male	White	2	Juxtaposition	6
Sydney	Greenleaf	Female	Hispanic	2	Juxtaposition	6
Amber	Azalea College	Female	African American	2	Hands-On	7
Dolores	Golden State	Female	African American	3	Hands-On	7
Elliot	Wabash	Male	White	1	Hands-On	7
Jade	St. Bernadette	Male	White	4	Hands-On	7
Beatriz	St. Bernadette	Female	Mexican American	4	Diversity and Identity	8
Diana	Golden State	Female	African American	2	Diversity and Identity	8
Owen	St. Bernadette	Male	White	4	Diversity and Identity	8

REFERENCES

Abes, E. S., Jones, S. R., & McEwen, M. K. (2007). Reconceptualizing the model of multiple dimensions of identity: The role of meaning-making capacity in the construction of multiple identities. *Journal of College Student Development, 48*(1), 1–22. Retrieved from https://doi.org/10.1353/csd.2007.0000

American College Personnel Association. (1996). *The student learning imperative.* Retrieved from http://www.myacpa.org/files/acpas-student-learning-imperative pdf

American Council on Education. (1937). *The student personnel point of view* (Vol. 1, No. 3). Washington DC: Author.

Association of American Colleges. (1991). *The challenge of connecting learning.* Available from Eric database. (ED328137)

Association of American Colleges & Universities. (n.d.). *Liberal education and America's promise.* Retrieved from https://www.aacu.org/leap

Association of American Colleges & Universities. (2002). *Greater expectations: A new vision for learning as a nation goes to college.* Retrieved from http://www.greaterexpectations.org/

Association of American Colleges & Universities. (2005). *Liberal education outcomes: A preliminary report on student achievement in college.* Washington DC: Author.

Association of American Colleges & Universities. (2007). *College learning for the new global century.* Washington DC: Author.

Association of American Colleges & Universities. (2008). *College learning for the new global century: Executive summary with employers' views on learning outcomes and assessment approaches.* Washington DC: Author.

Association of American Colleges & Universities. (2009). *Written communication VALUE rubric.* Retrieved from https://www.aacu.org/value/rubrics/written-communication

Association of American Colleges & Universities. (2010). *Integrative and applied learning value rubric.* Retrieved from https://www.aacu.org/value/rubrics/integrative-learning

Association of American Colleges & Universities. (2017). *Rising to the LEAP challenge: Case studies of integrative pathways to student signature work.* Retrieved from https://www.aacu.org/signaturework/publications

Association of American Colleges & Universities, & Carnegie Foundation. (2004). *A statement on integrative learning.* Washington DC: Author.

Barber, C. W. (2010). *Culture, surprise, and adaptation: Examining undergraduate students' matriculation processes* (Doctoral dissertation). Retrieved from http://commons.emich.edu/theses/270

REFERENCES

Barber, J. P. (2009). *Integration of learning: Meaning making for undergraduates through connection, application, and synthesis* (Doctoral dissertation). Available from ProQuest Dissertations and Theses database. (UMI No. 3354010)

Barber, J. P. (2012). Integration of learning: A grounded theory analysis of college students' learning. *American Educational Research Journal, 49*, 590–617. Retrieved from https://doi.org/10.3102/0002831212437854

Barber, J. P. (2014). Integration of learning model: How college students integrate learning. *New Directions for Higher Education, 16*, 7–17. Retrieved from https://doi.org/10.1002/he.20079

Barber, J. P., Barnhardt, C. L., & Young, R. L. (2017, November). *The power of integration: Undergraduate experiences that promote connections and translations beyond college.* Paper presented at the meeting of the Association for the Study of Higher Education, Houston, TX.

Barber, J. P., Bohon, L. L., & Everson, N. A. (2014, November). *Educators' voices: Examining the characteristics of integrative learning experiences.* Paper presented at the meeting of the Association for the Study of Higher Education, Washington DC.

Barber, J. P., & Bureau, D. A. (2012). Coming into focus: Positioning student learning from the student personnel point of view to today. In K. M. Boyle, J. W. Lowery, and J. A. Mueller (Eds.), *Reflections on the 75th anniversary of the student personnel point of view* (pp. 35–40). Washington DC: ACPA–College Student Educators International.

Barber, J. P., & King, P. M. (2014). Pathways toward self-authorship: Student responses to the demands of developmentally effective experiences. *Journal of College Student Development, 55*, 433–450. Retrieved from https://doi.org/10.1353/csd.2014.0047

Barr, R. B., & Tagg, J. (1995). From teaching to learning—A new paradigm for undergraduate education. *Change, 27*(6), 12–26. Retrieved from https://doi.org/10.1080/00091383.1995.10544672

Baxter Magolda, M. B. (1992). *Knowing and reasoning in college: Gender-related patterns in students' intellectual development.* San Francisco, CA: Jossey-Bass.

Baxter Magolda, M. B. (1999). *Creating contexts for learning and self-authorship: Constructive-developmental pedagogy.* Nashville, TN: Vanderbilt University Press.

Baxter Magolda, M. B. (2002). Helping students make their way to adulthood: Good company for the journey. *About Campus, 6*(6), 2–9. Retrieved from https://doi.org/10.1002/abc.66

Baxter Magolda, M. B. (2003). Identity and learning: Student affairs' role in transforming higher education. *Journal of College Student Development, 44*, 231–247. Retrieved from https://doi.org/10.1353/csd.2003.0020

Baxter Magolda, M. B. (2004a). Evolution of a constructivist conceptualization of epistemological reflection. *Educational Psychologist, 39*(1), 31–42. Retrieved from https://doi.org/10.1207/s15326985ep3901_4

Baxter Magolda, M. B. (2004b). *Making their own way: Narratives for transforming higher education to promote self-development.* Sterling, VA: Stylus.

Baxter Magolda, M. B. (2009). *Authoring your life: Developing an internal voice to navigate life's challenges*. Sterling, VA: Stylus.

Baxter Magolda, M. B., & King, P. M. (2004). *Learning partnerships: Theory and models of practice to educate for self-authorship*. Sterling, VA: Stylus.

Baxter Magolda, M. B., & King, P. M. (2007). Interview strategies for assessing self-authorship: Constructing conversations to assess meaning making. *Journal of College Student Development, 48*(5), 491–508. http://doi.org/10.1353/csd.2007.0055

Baxter Magolda, M. B., & King, P. M. (2012). Assessing meaning making and self-authorship: Theory, research, and application. *ASHE Higher Education Report, 38*(3). Retrieved from https://doi.org/10.1002/aehe.20003

Baxter Magolda, M. B., King, P. M., Taylor, K. B., and Wakefield, K. (2012). Decreasing authority dependence during the first year of college. *Journal of College Student Development, 53*, 418–435. Retrieved from https://doi.org/10.1353/csd.2012.0040

Berger, G. (1972). Introduction. In L. Apostel (Ed.), *Interdisciplinarity: Problems of teaching and research in universities* (pp. 21–26). Paris, France: Organisation for Economic Co-operation and Development.

Bingham, R. P., Bureau, D. A., & Duncan, A. G. (Eds.). (2015). *Leading assessment for student success: Ten tenets that change culture and practice in student affairs*. Sterling, VA: Stylus.

Bloom, B. S. (Ed.). (1956). *Taxonomy of educational objectives: The classification of educational goals by a committee of college and university examiners*. New York, NY: Longmans, Green.

Boes, L. (2006). *Learning from practice: A constructive-developmental study of undergraduate service-learning pedagogy* (Doctoral dissertation). Available from ProQuest Dissertations and Theses database. (UMI No. 3221585)

Boyer, E. L. (1987). *College: The undergraduate experience in America* (1st ed.). New York, NY: Harper & Row.

Boyer, E. L. (1990). *Scholarship reconsidered: Priorities of the professoriate*. Princeton, NJ: Carnegie Foundation for the Advancement of Teaching.

Brower, A. M., & Inkelas, K. K. (2010). Living-learning programs: One high-impact educational practice we now know a lot about. *Liberal Education, 96*(2), 36–43.

Brown, J. (2016). *The market logic in higher education: The changing organizational landscape at the beginning of the 21st century* (Doctoral dissertation). Retrieved from https://doi.org/10.18130/V3S57T

Brown Leonard, B. (2007). *Integrative learning as a developmental process: A grounded theory of college students' experiences in integrative studies* (Doctoral dissertation). Available from ProQuest Dissertations and Theses database. (UMI No. 3283405)

Cameron, J. (1992). *The artist's way: A spiritual path to higher creativity*. New York, NY: Putnam.

Carnevale, A. P., Smith, N., Melton, M., & Price, E. W. (2015). *Learning while earning: The new normal*. Retrieved from https://cew.georgetown.edu/cew-reports/workinglearners/

Collegiate Way. (2016). *The Yale report of 1828: Part 1*. Retrieved from http://collegiateway.org/reading/yale-report-1828/

Cuseo, J. B. (1998). Objectives and benefits of senior year programs. In J. N. Gardner, G. VanDerVeer, & Associates (Eds.), *The senior year experience: Facilitating integration, reflection, closure, and transition* (pp. 21–36). San Francisco, CA: Jossey-Bass.

Dewey, J. (1916). *Democracy and education: An introduction to the philosophy of education*. New York, NY: Macmillan.

Dewey, J. (1933). *How we think: A restatement of the relation of reflective thinking to the educative process*. Boston, MA: D. C. Heath.

Dewey, J. (1938). *Experience and education*. New York, NY: Macmillan.

DeZure, D., Babb, M., & Waldmann, S. (2005). Integrative learning nationwide: Emerging themes and practices. *Peer Review, 7*(3/4), 24–28.

Dirkx, J. M., Mezirow, J., & Cranton, P. (2006). Musings and reflections on the meaning, context, and process of transformative learning. *Journal of Transformative Education, 4*, 123–139. Retrieved from https://doi.org/10.1177/1541344606287503

Douglas, G. H. (1992). *Education without impact: How our universities fail the young*. New York, NY: Carol PubGroup.

Eagan, M. K., Stolzenberg, E. B., Zimmerman, H. B., Aragon, M. C., Whang Sayson, H., & Rios-Aguilar, C. (2017). *The American freshman: National norms fall 2016*. Retrieved from https://www.heri.ucla.edu/monographs/TheAmericanFreshman2016.pdf

Eodice, M., Geller, A. E., & Lerner, N. (2017). *The meaningful writing project: Learning, teaching and writing in higher education*. Logan: Utah State University Press.

Erikson, E. H. (1950). *Childhood and society*. New York, NY: Norton.

Evergreen State College. (n.d.). *Narrative evaluations*. Retrieved from https://www.evergreen.edu/evaluations

Eynon, B., & Gambino, L. M. (2017). *High-impact ePortfolio practice: A catalyst for student, faculty, and institutional learning*. Sterling, VA: Stylus.

Festinger, L. (1957). *A theory of cognitive dissonance*. Stanford, CA: Stanford University Press.

Fischer, K. W. (1980). A theory of cognitive development: The control and construction of hierarchies of skills. *Psychological Review, 87*, 477–531. Retrieved from https://doi.org/10.1037/0033-295X.87.6.477

Freire, P. (1970). *Pedagogy of the oppressed* (M. B. Ramos, Trans.). New York, NY: Continuum.

Gurin, P., Lehman, J. S., Lewis, E., Dey, E. L., Hurtado, S., & Gurin, G. (2004). *Defending diversity: Affirmative action at the University of Michigan*. Ann Arbor: University of Michigan Press.

Haynes, C. (2005, November). *Interdisciplinary terminology and theory*. Paper presented at the annual conference of the Association for the Study of Higher Education, Philadelphia, PA.

Hernández, D. M. (2018). *The actions institutional agents take to support first-generation Latino college students at a Catholic Hispanic-serving institution: An embedded case study* (Doctoral dissertation). Retrieved from http://dx.doi.org/10.25774/w4-pw64-h680

Hong, L., & Page, S. E. (2004). Groups of diverse problem solvers can outperform groups of high-ability problem solvers. *Proceedings of the National Academy of Sciences of the United States of America, 101*, 16385–16389. Retrieved from https://doi.org/10.1073/pnas.0403723101

Hopkins, L. T. (1937). *Integration, its meaning and application.* New York, NY: D. Appleton-Century.

Huber, M. T. (2020). *Teaching for liberal learning in higher education.* Washington DC, Association of American Colleges & Universities.

Huber, M. T., & Hutchings, P. (2004). *Integrative learning: Mapping the terrain.* Retrieved from https://www.aacu.org/publications-research/publications/integrative-learning-mapping-terrain

Inkelas, K. K., Jessup-Anger, J. E., Benjamin, M., & Wawrzynski, M. R. (2018). *Living-learning communities that work: A research-based model for design, delivery, and assessment.* Sterling, VA: Stylus.

Joint Task Force on Student Learning. (1998). *Powerful partnerships: A shared responsibility for learning.* Retrieved from https://www.aahea.org/articles/Jount_Task_Force.htm

Josselson, R. (1987). *Finding herself: Pathways to identity development in women.* San Francisco, CA: Jossey-Bass.

Judd, C. H. (1908). The relation of special training and general intelligence. *Educational Review, 36*, 28–42.

Judd, C. H. (1939). *Educational psychology.* New York, NY: Houghton Mifflin.

Kassens, A. L. (2014). Tweeting your way to improved #writing, #reflection, and #community. *Journal of Economic Education, 45*, 101–109. Retrieved from https://doi.org/10.1080/00220485.2014.889937

Kegan, R. (1994). *In over our heads: The mental demands of modern life.* Cambridge, MA: Harvard University Press.

Kelchen, R. (2018, May 29). A look at college students' living arrangements. Retrieved from https://robertkelchen.com/2018/05/28/a-look-at-college-students-living-arrangements/

Kerr, K. G., & Tweedy, J. (2006). Beyond seat time and student satisfaction: A curricular approach to residential education. *About Campus, 11*(5), 9–15. Retrieved from https://doi.org/10.1002/abc.181

Kerr, K. G., Tweedy, J., Edwards, K. E., & Kimmel, D. (2017). Shifting to curricular approaches to learning beyond the classroom. *About Campus, 22*(1), 22–31. Retrieved from https://doi.org/10.1002/abc.21279

King, P. M., & Baxter Magolda, M. B. (1996). A developmental perspective on learning. *Journal of College Student Development, 37*, 163–173.

King, P. M., Kendall Brown, M., Lindsay, N. K., & VanHecke, J. R. (2007). Liberal arts student learning outcomes: An integrated approach. *About Campus, 12*(4), 2–9. Retrieved from https://doi.org/10.1002/abc.222

King, P. M., & Kitchener, K. S. (1994). *Developing reflective judgment.* San Francisco, CA: Jossey-Bass.

King, P. M., Perez, R. J., & Shim, W. (2013). How college students experience intercultural learning: Key features and approaches. *Journal of Diversity in Higher Education, 6*(2), 69–83. Retrieved from https://doi.org/10.1037/a0033243

King, P. M., & Siddiqui, R. (2011). Self-authorship and metacognition: Related constructs for understanding college student learning and development. In C. Hoare (Ed.), *The Oxford handbook of reciprocal adult development and learning* (2nd ed., pp. 113–131). New York, NY: Oxford University Press.

King, P. M., & VanHecke, J. R. (2006). Making connections: Using skill theory to recognize how students build and rebuild understanding. *About Campus, 11*(1), 10–16.

Kitchener, K. S., & Fischer, K. W. (1990). *A skill approach to the development of reflective thinking* (Vol. 21). New York, NY: Karger.

Klein, J. T. (2005). Integrative learning and interdisciplinary studies. *Peer Review, 7*(4), 8–10.

Kolb, D. A. (1984). *Experiential learning: Experience as the source of learning and development.* Englewood Cliffs, NJ: Prentice-Hall, Inc.

Kraus, J. W. (1961). The development of a curriculum in the early American colleges. *History of Education Quarterly, 1*(2), 64–76. Retrieved from https://doi.org/10.2307/367641

Larkin, J. H. (1989). What kind of knowledge transfers? In L. B. Resnick (Ed.), *Knowing, learning and instruction: Essays in honor of Robert Glaser* (pp. 283–305). Hillsdale, NJ: Erlbaum.

Lattuca, L. R. (2001). *Creating interdisciplinarity: Interdisciplinary research and teaching among college and university faculty.* Nashville, TN: Vanderbilt University Press.

Lattuca, L. R., & Stark, J. S. (2009). *Shaping the college curriculum: Academic plans in context* (2nd ed.). San Francisco, CA: Jossey-Bass.

Leskes, A. (2004). Forword. In M. T. Huber and P. Hutchings, *Integrative learning: Mapping the terrain* (pp. iv–v). Washington DC: Association of American Colleges and Universities.

Letizia, A. J. (2016). Student writing for self-authorship and democracy: Engaging students critically. *Journal of College Student Development, 57,* 219–223. Retrieved from https://doi.org/10.1353/csd.2016.0017

Levine, A. (1998). A president's personal and historical perspective. In J. N. Gardner, G. VanDerVeer & Associates (Eds.), *The senior year experience: Facilitating integration, reflection, closure, and transition* (pp. 51–59). San Francisco, CA: Jossey-Bass.

Lipka, S. (2009, April 17). With "restorative justice," colleges strive to educate student offenders. *Chronicle of Higher Education.* Retrieved from https://www.chronicle.com/article/With-Restorative-Justice/30557

Love, P. G., & Guthrie, V. L. (1999). Synthesis, assessment, and application. *New Directions for Student Services, 88,* 77–93. Retrieved from https://doi.org/10.1002/ss.8807

Lumina Foundation. (2016). *Comprehensive student records. Learning happens everywhere.* Retrieved from https://www.luminafoundation.org/csr2025

Magolda, P. M., & Baxter Magolda, M. B. (Eds.). (2011). *Contested issues in student affairs: Diverse perspectives and respectful dialogue.* Sterling, VA: Stylus.

Magolda, P. M., Baxter Magolda, M. B., & Carducci R. (Eds.). (2019). *Contested issues in troubled times: Student affairs dialogues on equity, civility, and safety.* Sterling, VA: Stylus.

Marcia, J. E. (1966). Development and validation of ego-identity status. *Journal of Personality and Social Psychology, 3,* 551–558. Retrieved from https://doi.org/10.1037/h0023281

Maxwell, K. E., & Thompson, M. C. (2017). *Breaking ground through intergroup education: The program on intergroup relations (IGR) 1988–2016* (Working Paper 2017 No. 1). Retrieved from https://drive.google.com/file/d/14NDSVyIRerjEMUPln7BIjFIiIKZS9Ley/view

Mezirow, J. (1991). *Transformative dimensions of adult learning.* San Francisco, CA: Jossey-Bass.

Millner, M. (2018, February 12). Why I stopped writing on my students' papers. *Chronicle of Higher Education.* Retrieved from https://www.chronicle.com/article/Why-I-Stopped-Writing-on-My/242477

National Academies of Sciences, Engineering, and Medicine. (2018). *The integration of the humanities and arts with sciences, engineering, and medicine in higher education: Branches from the same tree.* Retrieved from https://doi.org/10.17226/24988

National Association of Student Personnel Administrators, & American College Personnel Administrators. (2004). *Learning reconsidered: A campus-wide focus on the student experience.* Retrieved from https://www.naspa.org/images/uploads/main/Learning_Reconsidered_Report.pdf

Niehaus, E., Holder, C., Rivera, M., Garcia, C. E., Woodman, T. C. & Dierberger, J. (2017). Exploring integrative learning in service-based alternative breaks. *Journal of Higher Education, 88*(6), 922–946. https://doi.org/10.1080/00221546.2017.1313086

National Center for Education Statistics. (2018). *IPEDS: Integrated Postsecondary Education Data System.* Retrieved from https://nces.ed.gov/ipeds/

National Research Council. (2015). *Enhancing the effectiveness of team science.* Washington DC: National Academies Press. Retrieved from https://doi.org/10.17226/19007

Newell, W. H. (2007). The role of interdisciplinary studies in the liberal arts. *LiberalArtsOnline, 7*(1), 245–255.

Newman, J. H. (1852). *The idea of a university.* South Bend, IN: Notre Dame University Press.

Pascarella, E. T, & Blaich, C. (2013). Lessons from the Wabash National Study of Liberal Arts Education. *Change, 45*(2), 6–15. Retrieved from https://doi.org/10.1080/00091383.2013.764257

Perez, R. J., & Barber, J. P. (2017). Intersecting outcomes: Promoting intercultural effectiveness and integration of learning for college students. *Journal of Diversity in Higher Education, 11*, 418–435. Retrieved from https://doi.org/10.1037/dhe0000067

Perez, R.J., Shim, W., King, P.M., & Baxter Magolda, M. B. (2015). Refining King and Baxter Magolda's model of intercultural maturity. *Journal of College Student Development 56*, 759–776. Retrieved from http://doi.10.1353/csd.2015.0085

Perkins, D., & Salomon, G. (1992). *Transfer of learning*. Retrieved from https://web.archive.org/web/20081203104029/http://learnweb.harvard.edu/alps/thinking/docs/traencyn.htm

Perry, W. G. (1970). *Forms of intellectual and ethical development in the college years: A scheme*. New York, NY: Holt, Rinehart and Winston.

Piaget, J. (1970). *Structuralism* (C. Maschler, Trans.). New York, NY: Basic Books.

Reynolds, C., & Patton, J. (2014). *Leveraging the ePortfolio for integrative learning: A faculty guide to classroom practices for transforming student learning*. Sterling, VA: Stylus.

Richards, D. A. (2017). *Skulls and keys: The hidden history of Yale's secret societies*. New York, NY: Pegasus Books.

Rogers, R. R. (2001). Reflection in higher education: A concept analysis. *Innovative Higher Education, 26*(1), 37–57. Retrieved from https://doi.org/10.1023/A:1010986404527

Schrage, J. M., & Giacomini, N. G. (Eds.). (2009). *Reframing campus conflict: Student conduct practice through a social justice lens*. Sterling, VA: Stylus.

Schwartz, M. S., & Fischer, K. W. (2006). Useful metaphors for tackling problems in teaching and learning. *About Campus, 11*(1), 2–9.

Seifert, T. A., Goodman, K., King, P. M., & Baxter Magolda, M. B. (2010). Using mixed methods to study first-year college impact on liberal arts learning outcomes. *Journal of Mixed Methods Research, 4*, 248–267. Retrieved from https://doi.org/10.1177/1558689810374960

Shapiro, S. L., Brown, K. W., & Astin, J. A. (2008). *Toward the integration of meditation into higher education: A review of research*. Retrieved from http://prsinstitute.org/downloads/related/spiritual-sciences/meditation/TowardtheIntegrationofMeditationintoHigherEducation.pdf

Shapiro, S. L., Carlson, L. E., Astin, J. A., & Freedman, B. (2006). Mechanisms of mindfulness. *Journal of Clinical Psychology, 62*, 373–386. Retrieved from https://doi.org/10.1002/jclp.20237

Sikes, A. M. (2018). *Rural students' experiences at selective four-year colleges: Pathways to persistence and success* (Doctoral dissertation). Retrieved from http://dx.doi.org/10.25774/w4-rjc7-rx48

Small, J. L. (2011). *Understanding college students' spiritual identities: Different faiths, varied worldviews*. New York, NY: Hampton Press.

Small, J. L., & Barber, J. P. (2019). Adding spirituality, religious diversity, and interfaith engagement to existing courses in student affairs preparation programs. In E. Patel, M. E. Geiss, & K. Goodman (Eds.), *A handbook for educating about religious diversity and interfaith engagement in student affairs* (pp. 74–89). Sterling, VA: Stylus.

Sobania, N., & Braskamp, L. A. (2009). Study abroad or study away: It's not merely semantics. *Peer Review, 11*(4), 23–26. Retrieved from https://www.aacu.org/publications-research/periodicals/study-abroad-or-study-away-its-not-merely-semantics

Stolzenberg, E. B., Eagan, M. K., Romo, E., Tamargo, E. J., Aragon, M. C., Luedke, M., & Kang, N. (2019). *The American freshman: National norms fall 2018*. Los Angeles, CA: Higher Education Research Institute. Retrieved from https://www.heri.ucla.edu/monographs/TheAmericanFreshman2018.pdf

Suskie, L. (2018). *Assessing student learning: A common sense guide* (3rd ed.). San Francisco, CA: Jossey-Bass.

Tang, Y.-Y., Ma, Y., Wang, J., Fan, Y., Feng, S., Lu, Q., . . . Posner, M. I. (2007). Short-term meditation training improves attention and self-regulation. *Proceedings of the National Academy of Sciences, 104*, 17152–17156. Retrieved from https://doi.org/10.1073/pnas.0707678104

Taylor, K. B., & Baker, A. R. (2019). Examining the role of discomfort in collegiate learning and development. *Journal of College Student Development, 60*, 173–188. Retrieved from https://doi.org/10.1353/csd.2019.0017

Thorndike, E. L. (1924). Mental discipline in high school studies. *Journal of Educational Psychology, 15*, 1–22, 83–98.

Thorndike, E. L., & Woodworth, R. S. (1901). The influence of improvement in one mental function upon the efficiency of other functions. *Psychological Review, 8*, 247–261.

Tuomi-Gröhn, T., & Engeström, Y. (2003). Conceptualizing transfer: From standard notions to developmental perspectives. In T. Tuomi-Gröhn & Y. Engeström (Eds.), *Between school and work: New perspectives on transfer and boundary-crossing* (pp. 19–38). Amsterdam, The Netherlands: Pergamon.

Umbach, P., & Wawrzynski, M. (2005). Faculty do matter: The role of college faculty in student learning and engagement. *Research in Higher Education, 46*, 153–184. Retrieved from https://doi.org/10.1007/s11162-004-1598-1

Useem, R. H., & Downie, R. D. (1976). Third-culture kids. *Today's Education, 65*(3), 103–105.

Voorhees, O. M. (1945). *The history of Phi Beta Kappa*. New York, NY: Crown.

Whitehead, A. N. (1929). *The aims of education, and other essays*. New York, NY: Macmillan.

Youngerman, E. (2018). Integrative learning in award-winning student writing: A grounded theory analysis. *AERA Open, 4*(3), 1–13. Retrieved from https://doi.org/10.1177/2332858418788825

Zaytoun, K. D. (2005). Identity and learning: The inextricable link. *About Campus, 9*(6), 8–15.

INDEX

AAC&U. *See* Association of American Colleges and Universities
academic advising, 10, 12, 44, 58–59, 65
academic affairs, 2
　culture of, 130
　student affairs and, 9–10, 22, 104
academic majors, 9, 20, 94, 130
academic papers, 65, 68
accreditation, 5, 135, 137, 140, 141
ACPA. *See* American College Personnel Association
aha moments, 147
alternative break experiences, 92, 93, 97, 103
Amber (study participant), 99
American Association of Collegiate Registrars and Admissions Officers, 142
American College Personnel Association (ACPA), 21, 22
American Council on Education, 21
application, 11, 25–26, 69
　across contexts, 33–34
　defined, 33
　embracing diversity and identity and, 114
　hands-on experiences and, 99
　juxtaposition and, 85–86
　mentoring and, 61
　writing and, 72–73

assessment. *See* integration of learning, documentation and assessment
Association of American Colleges and Universities (AAC&U), 14
　aims of, 19
　on connected learning, 15
　on integrative learning, 15
　on learning outcomes, 131
　on liberal education, 22
　on signature work, 134–35
　on writing, 67
Astin, J. A., 40, 42

banking concept of education, 21
Barber, J. P., 43, 112, 146
Baxter Magolda, M. B., 18, 28, 88
　on crossroads, 70, 86, 151
　on development domains, 150
　good company as guidance principle, 51–54
　learning partnerships model and, 117–18
　on meaning-making, 150
　self-authorship and, 70, 86, 149, 151
　on subject-object shift, 40
Beatriz (study participant), 105–6
Behind Closed Doors role-play, 103
Berger, G., 17
Black colleges, 106
blogs, 65, 76, 88
Bloom, B. S., 26
Boyer, E. L., 21

Brown, K. W., 40
Brown Leonard, B., 15

Cameron, J., 72
capstone experiences, 33, 44, 65, 134–35
Carducci, R., 88
Carlson, L. E., 42
Carnegie Foundation, 19
class discussions, 81, 87, 90–91
cognitive development, 39, 86, 150
cognitive dissonance
  juxtaposition and, 80, 84, 86
  tenets of, 83–84
Colin (study participant), 34
college educators, 1, 40, 52
  academic advising by, 58
  all inclusive term, 9–10
  defined, 2, 131
  ground rules and, 116
  integrative curriculum and, 123
  integrative lens and, 148
  knowledge for, 3
  missing opportunities, 13
  providing opportunities, 139
  questions of, 55
  strategies for, 4, 12
  work of, 128, 137, 147
common curriculum, 19
communication, 140
  across contexts, 141
  writing as, 69–70
concrete experience, 97
confidence building, 57
conflicts, 56
  external and internal, 151
  reconciliation of, 4, 29, 79, 80, 95
connected learning, 14, 15, 16
connection, 11, 25–26, 69

defined, 33
embracing diversity and identity and, 113
establishment of, 32–33
hands-on experiences and, 98–99
juxtaposition and, 85
mentoring and, 60–61
writing and, 72
consciousness, five orders of, 149
conversations, 55, 142
cross-disciplinary perspectives, 131
crossroads, 70, 84, 86, 132, 151

daily life, 44, 77, 93–95, 99, 100, 104
debates, 21, 68, 89, 90
development
  developmental theories, 86, 88
  dimensions and domains of, 150–51
  of integration of learning model, 25–26
  in integrative curriculum, 132
  intellectual development, 40
  link with learning, 30–32
  meaning-making holistic view of, 149–50
  self-authorship as framework, 149
devil's advocate, 87–88
Dewey, John, 20–21, 32, 111
  on reflection, 37
Diana (study participant), 114–15
difficult retreat, 94–95
disciplinary curriculum outcomes, 130–31
disorienting dilemmas, 94, 103
disparate learners, 128–29
dissonance, 4, 79, 83. *See also* cognitive dissonance

diversity, 4, 46, 83. *See also* embracing diversity and identity
documentation. *See* integration of learning, documentation and assessment
Dolores (study participant), 100
Downie, R. D., 101
dreaming, 41

eating disorders, 103
ego identity statuses, 88
Elliot (study participant), 34, 96
e-mails, 38, 58, 63, 65, 118
embracing diversity and identity, 139
  application and, 114
  connection and, 113
  diverse learning environments for, 106–7
  educator's identity in, 117
  gender and, 106, 108
  ground rules in, 116
  IGR and, 110–11, 113
  in integration of learning, 108–9
  in integration of learning model, 113–15
  in integrative curriculum, 126
  intentional groups and paring in, 116
  multiple dimensions of identity model and, 108–10
  overview, 105–6
  recruiting for diversity, 118
  reflection in, 111–13
  reflective questions for, 119
  strategies for, 116–18
  student experiences, 115
  student home and childhood experiences in, 117
  student identities in, 107–8
  student prior learning in, 117–18
  summary, 118–19
  synthesis and, 114–16
  in Wabash National Study of Liberal Arts Education, 108
Engeström, Y., 38
Eodice, M., 67
epistemological reflection, 40
Erikson, E. H., 88
Ethan (study participant), 44–46
ethnicity, 116
  ethnic groups, 88
examinations, 20
experimental education, 20–21
experimentation, 97, 98, 134
exploratory factor analysis, 146

face-to-face meetings, 60, 77, 101. *See also* one-on-one meetings
faith, 61, 97, 116, 131
  faith-based institutions, 42–43, 106, 112–13
feedback, 67, 73, 77
  formative and summative, 144–46
  on portfolios, 143–44
Festinger, L., 83–84
fight or flight, 94
Fischer, K. W., 17–18
Fisler, Jodi, 137
focus groups, 141–42
formative feedback, 144–46
Fran (study participant), 13, 23
Freedman, B., 42
free writing, 70, 72, 74–75
Freire, Paolo, 21, 111
funding, 5, 137

Gavin (study participant), 42–43
Geller, A. E., 67

gender, 117. *See also* sexuality
  in embracing diversity and
    identity, 106, 108
  mentoring and, 59
  syllabus and, 90
general principles concept, 38,
  151–52
Georgetown University Center on
  Education and Workforce, 96
goals
  of integration of learning, 2
  integrative learning goals, 138–39
  for mentoring, 63
good company as guidance
  principle, 51–52
great accommodation, 40
grounded theory approach, 3
ground rules, 116
group discussions, 79, 87
Guthrie, V. L., 40

hands-on experiences, 4, 139
  application and, 99
  characteristics of, 94
  connection and, 98–99
  disorienting dilemmas for, 94,
    103
  engaging multiple senses, 102
  integration of learning and,
    94–95
  in integration of learning model,
    98–101
  in integrative curriculum, 126
  maker spaces and, 102
  overview, 92–93
  reflection and, 95–98
  reflective questions for, 104
  regular opportunities for, 101
  relevance of, 101
  role-playing in, 103
  space and place for, 102
  strategies for, 101–3
  student experiences, 93, 98
  summary, 103
  synthesis and, 99–101
Hernández, D. M., 55
Higham, John, 20
higher education
  barriers in, 3
  borders in, 9
  integrative learning as outcome,
    10
  need for worldview in, 43
  outcomes, 1
  promotion by, 23
  as self-perpetuating, 52
  thriving on juxtaposition, 82
  Virginia State Council of Higher
    Education, 137
  writing as cornerstone, 67
Hopkins, L. T., 14
Horton, Myles, 111
human resources, 5, 137

identical elements concept, 38,
  151–52
identity, 4. *See also* embracing
    diversity and identity
  ego identity statuses, 88
  learning and, 31
  relevance of, 88
  worldview, 112
IGR. *See* intergroup relations
immersive experiences, 4, 67, 93,
  95, 97
inclusive transcripts, 142–43
Inman, Ann Leslie, 53–54, 61–62
innovation, 134
institutional agents, as mentoring
  guides, 55–56
integrated core, 21
integration of learning

assessment of, 4–5
background of, 5
barriers to, 3
concrete and abstract methods, 12
definitions for, 14–15
documenting, 4–5
as educational outcome, 16, 18
embracing diversity and identity in, 108–9
enthusiasm for, 13
goals of, 2
good company as guidance principle in, 52
hands-on experiences and, 94–95
as higher education outcome, 10
as integrative practices, 15–18
juxtaposition and, 81
learning partnerships model and, 52
meaning-making and, 110
personal connection to, 10–12
reflective questions for, 23
research, 5
role of mentoring, 54–55
strategies for, 3
student mastery of, 5
student success through, 2
subject-object shift as integral to, 40
summary, 22–23
teaching and assessment of, 1
transfer and, 18
transparency in, 1
writing as praxis, 66–67
integration of learning, documentation and assessment approaches to, 141–48
communication across contexts, 141
formative and summative feedback in, 144–46
inclusive transcripts for, 142–43
Integration of Learning Assessment Cycle, 138–41
interviews and focus groups for, 141–42
overview, 137–38
portfolios for, 143–44
quantitative scale for, 146
reflective questions for, 148
rubrics for, 146–47
summary, 148
temporal lag and, 146–48
Integration of Learning Assessment Cycle
assessment of student integration of learning, 139–40
establishment of integrative learning goals, 138–39
providing opportunities for integrative learning, 139
results for improving integration of learning, 140–41
integration of learning model. *See also* application; connection; synthesis
background for, 24
definition of, 11–12
development of, 25–26
embracing diversity and identity in, 113–15
fluidity in, 69
grounded theory approach, 3
hands-on experiences in, 98–101
juxtaposition in, 84–87
learning categories, 25–26, 32–35
link between development and learning, 30–32
mentoring in, 60–62

INDEX

reflective questions for, 35–36
relevance of, 36
summary, 35
Wabash National Study of Liberal Arts Education and, 26–30
what it is not, 26
writing in, 71–74
integrative body-mind training, 42
integrative curriculum, 4, 115
blank planning matrix, 127
capstone experiences in, 134–35
cocurricular outcomes, 131
college educators and, 123
cross-disciplinary perspectives and outcomes, 131
developmental considerations, 132
disciplinary curriculum outcomes, 130–31
disparate learners and, 128–29
embracing diversity and identity in, 126
experimentation and innovation in, 134
foothold and opportunity in, 123
hands-on experiences in, 126
integrative lens for, 129, 130
intercontextual curriculum concept, 16, 18, 130–32, 141
intercontextual outcomes, 131
involving all curriculum, 123
juxtaposition in, 125
mentoring in, 125
menu approach, 132–33
model for, 123–24
overview, 123–27
partners in, 124
planning matrix for, 125–26
quality of, 124
reflective questions for, 136
scaffolding in, 133–34
self-designed assignments in, 133
signature work in, 134–35
strategies for, 132–35
summary, 135
transparency in, 133
writing in, 125
integrative learning, 1, 3, 5
AAC&U on, 15
attention toward, 23
integrative lens, 91, 129, 130, 136, 148
integrative practices, 15–18
history of, 19–22
integrative processes, 19
intellectual development, 40
intentional groups and paring, 116
intercollegiate athletics, 82, 93, 130
intercontextual curriculum concept, 16, 18, 130–32, 141
interdisciplinarity, 16–18, 82
intergroup relations (IGR), 110–11, 113
internships, 93, 96, 130, 145
interpersonal development, 39, 150
interviews
for documentation and assessment, 141–42
reflection through, 44–46
in Wabash National Study of Liberal Arts Education, 13, 28–30, 142
intradisciplinarity, 16–17
intrapersonal development, 39, 150

Jade (study participant), 96–97
Johns Hopkins University, 20
journaling, 65, 66, 70, 74
Judd, Charles, 38, 151–52
juxtaposition, 4
aggregative and integrative approaches for, 81–83

application and, 85–86
cognitive dissonance and, 80, 84, 86
compare and contrast aspect, 81
connection and, 85
demonstration, 90
devil's advocate for, 87–88
higher education thriving on, 82
integration of learning and, 81
in integration of learning model, 84–87
in integrative curriculum, 126
intentional practice for, 88–89
meaning-making and, 83
overview, 79–80
reflection in, 83–84
reflective questions for, 91
in residential programs, 82–83
restorative justice initiatives as, 80
student experience, 86
summary, 90–91
syllabus for, 90
synthesis and, 86–87

Kayla (study participant), 44–46
Kegan, R., 40, 42, 70
Kerr, K. G., 123–24
King, P. M., 18, 28, 39, 40, 103
  on meaning-making, 150
Kitchener, K. S., 40, 103
knowledge economy, 10
Kolb, D. A., 97

Lattuca, L. R., 17, 123
learner-centered pedagogies, 111
learning, 1
  AAC&U on outcomes, 131
  awareness of, 39–40
  connected learning, 14, 15, 16
  disparate learners, 128–29

formal and informal, 24
identity and, 31
Judd on, 151–52
link with development, 30–32
outside classroom, 9
Thorndike on, 151–52
three things to know, 2
transfer of, 18, 151–52
transformative learning, 94, 103
learning partnerships model, 52, 117–18
Lerner, N., 67
Letizia, A. J., 70
LGBTQ groups, 88, 111
Liberal Education and America's Promise project, 22
life experiences, 2, 10, 20
living-learning communities, 4, 82–83, 92–93, 95, 102
Love, P. G., 40
Lumina Foundation, 142–43

Magolda, P. M., 88
maker spaces, 4, 102, 103
Marcia, J. E., 88
Matt (study participant), 79–80
Maxwell, K. E., 111
meaning-making
  Baxter Magolda on, 150
  breaking into smaller parts, 32
  cognition and, 39
  external and internal continuum, 151
  holistic view of development, 149–50
  integration of learning and, 110
  juxtaposition and, 83
  King on, 150
  in multiple dimensions of identity model, 109
  portfolios and, 71

Wabash National Study of Liberal
    Arts Education and, 29–30,
    146
  writing in, 65, 66, 69–70
meditation
  metacognition and, 42
  as reflection, 42–43
  relevance and, 42
mentoring, 3–4
  advising compared to, 58
  application and, 61
  being realistic about, 63
  benefits for mentor, 58–59
  connection and, 60–61
  defining relationships in, 63
  goals for, 63
  good company as guidance
    principle, 51–54
  instigation of, 54
  institutional agents as guides,
    55–56
  in integration of learning model,
    60–62
  in integrative curriculum, 125
  intentional selection for, 62
  mentors as confidence builders,
    57
  mentors as conscience, 57
  office hours compared to, 58
  overview, 51
  questions for, 56
  racial and gender dynamics, 59
  referral strategy, 59
  reflection and, 56–57
  reflective questions for, 63–64
  relationship building, 59
  role in integration of learning,
    54–55
  scheduled interactions for, 62
  strategies for, 62–63
  student experience, 60–62
  summary, 63
  synthesis and, 61–62
  varied forms of, 62
  Wabash National Study of Liberal
    Arts Education and, 51, 62
menu approach to integrative
    curriculum, 132–33
metacognition, 39–40, 41
  meditation and, 42
  reflection and, 68
Mezirow, J., 39, 94, 103
  on reflection, 37–38
Millner, M., 145–46
mindfulness, 42
mind mapping, 76
moral reasoning, 103
morning pages, 72
multidisciplinarity, 17
multiple dimensions of identity
    model, 108–10

narratives, 143
NASPA. *See* National Association
    of Student Personnel
    Administrators
National Academies of Sciences,
    Engineering, and Medicine,
    81–82
National Association of Student
    Personnel Administrators
    (NASPA), 22, 142
Nick (study participant), 32–33
Niehaus, 97

office hours, 44, 58, 61
one-on-one meetings, 12, 24, 41,
    61, 62, 63, 65
organization membership, 130
Owen (study participant), 113

passive programming, 89
Patton, J., 144
Perez, R. J., 112
Perkins, D., 152
Perry, W. G., 32, 40, 86, 149–50
perspective taking, 111–12
Piaget, J., 32
Plato, 13
pluridisciplinarity, 17
Poland, 92–93, 100
policymakers, 135, 140
portfolios, 65
    e-Portfolio system, 144
    feedback on, 143–44
    for integration of learning, documentation and assessment, 143–44
    meaning-making and, 71
    writing in action, 71
prayer, 42–43

quantitative scale, 146
quiet mind, 38–39

race, 90, 108, 109, 116, 117
    mentoring and, 59
    racial groups, 88
reading lists, 90
reflection, 3, 23
    definitions of, 37–38
    Dewey, on, 37
    in embracing diversity and identity, 111–13
    epistemological reflection, 40
    hands-on experiences and, 95–98
    in juxtaposition, 83–84
    meditation and prayer as, 42–43
    mentoring and, 56–57
    metacognition and, 39–40, 68
    Mezirow on, 37–38
    overview, 37–38
    practices of, 40–41
    questions, 46–47
    quiet mind and, 38–39
    reflective dreaming, 41
    reflective talking, 41
    reflective thinking, 41
    reflective walking, 41
    through reminding, scheduling, responding, 43–44
    summary, 46
    through Wabash National Study of Liberal Arts Education interviews, 44–46
    in writing, 41, 69–71, 74–75
reflective judgment, 40
relationships
    building, in mentoring, 59
    defining, in mentoring, 63
relevance
    of faith, 112
    of hands-on experiences, 101
    of identity, 88
    of integration of learning model, 36
    of knowledge, 18
    meditation and, 42
    of past experiences, 117
    writing and, 67
reperceiving, 42
residential programs, 82–83, 93, 130
restorative justice initiatives, 80
Reynolds, C., 144
Rogers, R. R., 38
role-playing, 103
rubrics, 146–47

Salomon, G., 152
scaffolding, in integrative curriculum, 133–34

self, 18, 45, 52, 108
self-authorship, 5, 84
    Baxter Magolda and, 70, 86, 149, 151
    as development framework, 149
    holistic nature of, 39–40
    Wabash National Study of Liberal Arts Education and, 29–30, 34
self-confidence, 103
self-designed assignments, 133
self-harm, 103
self-regulation, 42
self-transformation, 149
service-oriented study, 97
sexual assault, 103
sexuality, 90, 106, 108, 109, 116, 117
Shapiro, S. L., 40, 42
Siddiqui, R., 39
signature work, 134–35
skill theory, 17–18
Small, J. L., 43
small group work, 24, 77, 80, 114, 116
spirituality, 43
standardized tests, 138
Stark, J. S., 123
student affairs, 2
    academic affairs and, 9–10, 22, 104
    activities of, 110
    culture of, 130
students. *See also* development
    embracing diversity and identity experiences, 115
    hands-on experiences, 93, 98
    home and childhood experiences of, 117
    identities, in embracing diversity and identity, 107–8
    juxtaposition experience, 86
    life experiences, 10
    mastery of integrative learning, 5
    mentoring experience, 60–62
    prior learning and, 117–18
    success through integrative learning, 2
    writing experience, 72
study abroad, 81, 89–90, 92–95, 130
    synthesis and, 100–101
study away, 89, 92–95, 130
    service-oriented, 97
subject-object shift, 40, 42
summative feedback, 144–46
Sydney (study participant), 85
synthesis, 11, 25–26, 69
    defined, 33
    embracing diversity and identity and, 114–16
    hands-on experiences and, 99–101
    juxtaposition and, 86–87
    mentoring and, 61–62
    of new whole, 34–35
    study abroad and, 100–101
    worldview and, 61
    writing and, 73–74, 128

talking, 41
Tang, Y.-Y., 42
team science, 22
temporal lag, 146–48
term educator, 124
thinking, 41
Thompson, M. C., 111
Thorndike, Edward, 38, 151–52
transdisciplinarity, 17
transfer of learning, 18, 151–52
transformative learning, 94, 103
transparency
    in integration of learning, 1

in integrative curriculum, 133
Tuomi-Gröhn, T., 38
Tweedy, J., 123
tweeting, 41, 65, 75–76
Tyler (study participant), 66, 73–74

unified curriculum, 20
University of Michigan, 20
Useem, R. H., 101

values, 19, 39, 57, 108, 112, 140
VanHecke, J. R., 18
Virginia Sate Council of Higher Education, 137

Wabash National Study of Liberal Arts Education, 1, 3–4
  for advancing knowledge of learning, 141
  Amber (study participant), 99
  analysis, 12
  Beatriz (study participant), 105–6
  Colin (study participant), 34
  conversations and, 55
  developmental pathways found, 94
  development domains and, 150
  Diana (study participant), 114–15
  Dolores (study participant), 100
  Elliot (study participant), 34, 96
  embracing diversity and identity in, 108
  Ethan (study participant), 44–46
  follow-up in, 140
  four-year design of, 149
  Fran (study participant), 13, 23
  Gavin (study participant), 42–43
  group discussions in, 79
  institutional contexts, 26–27
  integration of learning model and, 26–30
  interviews, 13, 28–30, 142, 150
  Jade (study participant), 96–97
  Kayla (study participant), 44–46
  longitudinal nature of, 27
  Matt (study participant), 79–80
  meaning-making and, 29–30, 146
  mentoring and, 51, 62
  Nick (study participant), 32–33
  Owen (study participant), 113
  qualitative data from, 54, 146
  reflection through interviews, 44–46
  research team and data, 11, 23
  residential experience and, 95
  self-authorship and, 29–30, 34
  skill of silence for, 56
  study abroad in, 81, 92
  Sydney (study participant), 85
  Tyler (study participant), 66, 73–74
  Wallace (study participant), 68–69
walking, 41
Wallace (study participant), 68–69
Whitehead, Alfred, 20
word association, 76–77
workforce, 10
workshopping, 77
work study, 22, 53, 62, 96, 130
worldview, 39, 106, 108, 129, 131
  in higher education, 43
  identity, 112
  synthesis and, 61
writing, 4
  AAC&U on, 67
  application and, 72–73
  as communication, 69–70
  conferences, 77

connection and, 72
across contexts, 67–68
framework for, 70
free writing, 70, 72, 74–75
by hand, 75
as higher education cornerstone, 67
in integration of learning model, 71–74
in integrative curriculum, 125
in meaning-making, 65, 66, 69–70
overview, 65–66
portfolios in action, 71
praxis in integration of learning, 66–67
reflection in, 41, 69–71, 74–75
reflective questions for, 78
relevance and, 67
strategies for, 74–77
student experience in, 72
summary, 77
synthesis and, 73–74, 128
teaching of, 65–66
Tyler (study participant) on, 66, 73–74
Wallace (study participant) on, 68–69
Youngerman on, 67–68, 73, 74

Yale Report of 1828, 19–20
Youngerman, E., 67–68, 73, 74

Zaytoun, K. D., 31
Zen meditation, 42

For Product Safety Concerns and Information please contact our EU
representative GPSR@taylorandfrancis.com
Taylor & Francis Verlag GmbH, Kaufingerstraße 24, 80331 München, Germany

www.ingramcontent.com/pod-product-compliance
Lightning Source LLC
Chambersburg PA
CBHW071411300426
44114CB00016B/2257